The World's Dreamiest Beaches

The World's
Dreamiest Beaches

Preface

"The sea is the last free place on earth." The man who made this remark must have known what he was talking about, for Ernest Hemingway spent half his life on and by the Caribbean Sea. And he was right! Nothing compares to the indescribable feeling of freedom and contentment that a person experiences while gazing calmly across the endless blue expanse of the sea as it stretches way out to the horizon. One feels almost magically drawn to it.

The sea is the source of all life on earth, and yet nothing is as secretive as the sea with so many bizarre creatures hidden in its depths. It is, therefore, little wonder that large numbers of myths have grown up around the ocean or that tales of the sea have become popular motifs in art, music and literature since time immemorial.

Over three-quarters of the surface of our planet consists of oceans, seas and rivers whose coastal areas are more than 280,000 kilometres in length. So there's enough room for everyone to find his or her very own favourite beach. The mere mention of the word, "beach paradise", makes most people think of summer, sun and sand. This is especially true since Coco Chanel made tanning popular in the 1920s and tanned skin came to be ideal beauty worth striving for.

This book invites you on a trip to the most beautiful coastlines on Earth. In the process, you'll encounter beaches in Thailand with sand as fine as powdered sugar, red and black lava beaches on the Canary Islands, Scandinavia's stony fjords, picturesque seashores in New Zealand, and palm-lined, sunny Caribbean paradises. You'll travel to wide California beaches, the bright red cliffs of Portugal, and pristine South Sea islands. And you may well be mesmerised by Australia's brilliantly white sands, South Africa's soft dunes, and the world famous beaches of Rio de Janeiro.

Our travel destinations are divided into seven chapters. At the start of each chapter, a map with a legend will help you to follow the route with your finger as you travel along with us. The arrangement of countries and beaches is broadly based on a north-south course, which then proceeds along the respective coastlines. The selection of dreamy beaches cannot possibly be complete, nor would we wish it to be; rather, it provides an incentive for readers to go on their own journey of discovery. Just as every ocean is different from every other, so too are our planet's coastlines and shores incredibly varied and sensationally beautiful. Such diversity whets your appetite for the shore, so let the words and pictures tempt you. We hope you'll give your wanderlust free reign!

Contents

Europe

Asia

Africa

North and Central America

Australia and Oceania

The Caribbean

South America

EUROPE

FABULOUS NATURE AND CULTURAL ABUNDANCE

According to Greek mythology, Europe was the daughter of a king who was abducted by Zeus to the Island of Crete. So it was that a young girl playing on the beach gave her name to a continent that offers the most diverse landscapes and coastlines from Sicily to Norway and the Atlantic to the Baltic. The old continent is richly blessed with natural wonders. The cliffs of Ireland, Denmark's sprawling dunes, and Iceland's seaside glaciers and geysers work their austere, northern charms. All across southern Europe's Mediterranean, the beauty of nature is reflected in above ground caves, grottoes and cliffs, and in fascinating underwater preserves. The change of seasons also lends exceptional splendour to the landscape. From Spanish almond blossoms to the wintry charm of Scandinavian fjords, Europe has something for every taste. And her many-faceted beaches, dark forests, impressive cliffs, matchless cities of antiquity, and sophisticated spa resorts are always at the ready. It is always springtime on Gran Canaria, Tenerife and Lanzarote. European sun worshippers flock year round to the richly varied beaches, extinct volcanoes, and mild climate of the Canary Islands.

European Beaches

1	Grundarfjördur	57	Barguzinsky Bay, Lake Baikal	112	Mont-Saint-Michel Bay, Manche
2	Jökulsarlon	58	Sochi, Southern Russia	113	Saint-Malo, Ille-et-Vilaine
3	Oyarbakki	59	Buarcos, Coimbra	114	Crozon, Finistère
4	Magdalena Fjord, Spitzbergen	60	Cascais, Estremadura	115	Saint Tugen, Finistère
5	Sommarøy, Troms	61	Praia de Amoreira, The Algarve	116	Dune du Pyla, Gironde
6	Andøya, Vesterålen	62	Zavial, The Algarve	117	Biarritz, Pyrénées- Atlantiques
7	Utakleiv, Lofoten	63	Ponta da Piedade, The Algarve	118	Saint-Tropez, Côte d'Azur
8	Mandal, West Agder	64	Praia do Camilo, The Algarve	119	Cannes, Côte d'Azur
9	Gotland, Götaland	65	Praia Dona Ana, The Algarve	120	Nice, Côte d'Azur
10	Stora Nassa, Stockholm	66	Praia da Rocha, The Algarve	121	Menton, Côte d'Azur
11	Rauma, Western Finland	67	Prainha, The Algarve	122	Désert des Agriates, Corsica
12	Achill Island, Connaught	68	Praia do Três Irmãos, The Algarve	123	Palombaggia, Corsica
13	Inch, Kerry	69	Benagil, The Algarve	124	Lido di Jesolo, The Veneto
14	Seilebost Beach, Isle of Harris	70	Praia da Marinha, The Algarve	125	Rimini, Emilia-Romagna
15	Newquay, Cornwall	71	Praia Sao Rafael, The Algarve	126	Punta della Contessa, Elba
16	Durdle Door, Dorset	72	Albufeira, The Algarve	127	Marina di Alberese, Tuscany
17	Brighton, East Sussex	73	Praia da Falésia, The Algarve	128	Baia delle Zagare, Apulia
18	L'Ancresse Bay, Guernsey	74	Caniçal, Madeira	129	Capri, Campania
19	Portelet Bay, Jersey	75	Porto Santo	130	Positano, Campania
20	Oostduinkerke, West Flanders	76	Playa de Las Catedrales, Costa de Lugo	131	Tropea, Calabria
21	Scheveningen, The Hague	77	Playa Cuevas del Mar, Costa Verde	132	Capo Vaticano, Calabria
22	Zandvoort, North Holland			133	Lipari, Aeolian Islands
23	De Koog, Texel	78	Llanfranc, Costa Brava	134	Giardini Naxos, Sicily
24	Schiermonnikoog National Park	79	Tossa de Mar, Costa Brava	135	Cefalù, Sicily
25	Rømø, Southern Denmark	80	Lloret de Mar, Costa Brava	136	Lampedusa, Pelagic Islands
26	Jutland	81	Sant Pol de Mar, Costa Brava	137	Spiaggia del Principe, Sardinia
27	Løkken, North Jutland	82	Benidorm, Costa Blanca	138	Bari Sardo, Sardinia
28	Ærø, Southern Denmark	83	Marbella, Costa del Sol	139	Is Arutas, Sardinia
29	Møn, Zealand	84	Tarifa, Costa de la Luz	140	Chia, Sardinia
30	Dueodde, Bornholm	85	Cala Galdana, Menorca	141	Porto Campana, Sardinia
31	Borkum	86	Binibèquer, Menorca	142	Golden Bay, Malta
32	Juist	87	Cap de Formentor, Majorca	143	Ramla Bay, Gozo
33	Norderney	88	Alcúdia, Majorca	144	Murter, Sibenik-Knin
34	Langeoog	89	Cala Mondragó, Majorca	145	Donja Brela, Split-Dalmatia
35	Spiekeroog	90	Andraitx, Majorca	146	Braã, Split-Dalmatia
36	Heligoland	91	Cala Salada, Ibiza	147	Dubrovnik, Dubrovnik-Neretva
37	St. Peter-Ording, Schleswig-Holstein	92	Playa d'en Bossa, Ibiza	148	Paleokastritsa, Corfu
38	Westerland, Sylt	93	Playa de Ses Illetes, Formentera	149	Lassi, Kefalonia
39	Red Cliffs, Sylt	94	Playa Francesca, La Graciosa	150	Navagio, Zakynthos
40	Fehmarn	95	El Golfo, Lanzarote	151	Elafonisos, The Peloponnese
41	Timmendorf Beach, Schleswig-Holstein	96	Playa Blanca, Lanzarote	152	Balos, Crete
42	Travemünde, Schleswig-Holstein	97	Playas de Papagayo, Lanzarote	153	Matala, Crete
43	Kühlungsborn, Mecklenburg-Western Pomerania	98	Playa de Corralejo, Fuerteventura	154	Sarakiniko, Milos
44	Prerow, Mecklenburg- Western Pomerania	99	Costa Calma, Fuerteventura	155	Mykonos, Cyclades
45	Hiddensee	100	Playa de Sotavento, Fuerteventura	156	Agia Anna, Amorgos
46	Binz, Rügen	101	Morro Jable, Fuerteventura	157	Faliraki, Rhodes
47	Ahlbeck, Usedom	102	Playa del Inglés, Gran Canaria	158	Kira Panagia, Karpathos
48	Wannsee, Berlin	103	Maspalomas, Gran Canaria	159	Lalaria, Skiathos
49	Tihany, Lake Balaton	104	Playa de las Teresitas, Tenerife	160	Sithonia, Halkidiki
50	Niechorze, Western Pomerania	105	Playa de la Arena, Tenerife	161	Bolata, Dobrudja
51	Curonian Spit	106	Playa de las Americas, Tenerife	162	Sinemorets, Burgas
52	Curonian Lagoon	107	Valle Gran Rey, La Gomera	163	Constanta
53	Jurmala	108	Puerto Naos, La Palma	164	Mamaia
54	Livonia	109	Playa del Verodal, El Hierro	165	Bodrum, Mugla
55	Pärnu	110	Étretat, Seine-Maritime	166	Marmaris, Mugla
56	Võsu, Lahemaa National Park	111	Cabourg, Calvados	167	Blue Lagoon, Oludeniz
				168	Kaputas, Antalya
				169	Cleopatra Beach, Alanya
				170	Golden Sands
				171	Famagusta
				172	Asterias Beach

Iceland

Grundarfjörður *(above)*

Western Iceland's Snæfellsnes Peninsula is a mystical place. So it comes as no surprise that Jules Verne's hero descends into the legendary volcano, Snæfellsjökull, in *Journey to the Centre of the Earth*. The majestic glacier, mountain landscapes, often turbulent, deep blue sea, and charming Westfjords of the little harbour city of Grundarfjörður make quite an impression.

Jökulsarlon *(below)*

South Iceland's top attraction, the Jökulsarlon Glacial Lagoon, is a natural setting of magical beauty. Two James Bond films were filmed here on location. While cruising the lagoons, you can almost reach out and touch the icebergs. An impressive black lava beach lies at the point where the North Sea flows into the Atlantic. You can take a stroll here among gigantic, beached chunks of ice.

The Faroes

Oyarbakki
(above)

The combination of fjords, green, treeless swathes of land, and cliffs rising steeply out of the sea make the Faroe Islands one of Northern Europe's natural wonders. The hamlet of Oyarbakki is located between Streymoy and Eysturoy. From here, visitors can head out on hikes in the secluded mountains or admire colonies of sea birds perched between clouds and water.

Norway

Magdalena Fjord, Spitzbergen
(centre)

Spitzbergen gets its name from its sharply towering, needle-like mountain peaks.
The steep ice walls, grandiose glaciers, and glassy waters of Magdalena Fjord lie in the midst of this majestic scenery. With a bit of luck, you may spot minke whales and seals swimming by the drifting ice floes.

Sommarøy, Troms
(below)

The islands of Sommarøy and Hillerøy are in Northern Norway, about forty-five minutes by car from Tromsø. They are surrounded by countless little islands and islets that present a beautiful panorama, especially at sunset. This is where you'll find one sheltered bay after another with sandy, snow-white beaches. In winter, the Northern Lights transform Sommarøy into a surreal landscape.

Utakleiv, Lofoten (above)

You'll get an overwhelming panoramic view of the steep mountains and the North Sea from Utakleiv Beach in Norway's Lofoten Islands. Sandy white beaches invite you on extended strolls, and the striking fjord landscape inspires you to hike in the mountains. Killer whales are a big draw, and visitors come to the region every autumn to watch them.

Mandal, West Agder (centre)

Mandal is Norway's southernmost city. Its origins date back to around 1500 CE, when it developed as a terminal for the country's chief export, wood. Wood even shaped the townscape: about 650 wooden houses in the narrow side streets of the town centre are currently listed on the historic register. Beautiful Sjøsanden Beach is located right nearby. You can play volleyball on the wide, sandy beach or simply enjoy the sun and sea.

Andøya, Vesterålen (below)

Vesterålen lies 300 km north of the Arctic Circle. This island group has lots of Nordic charm in unspoilt natural surroundings. Vesterålen Beach lies in the spot where the mountains seem to plunge into the sea, visitors go on whale watching tours and, depending on the time of year, the Northern Lights or the midnight sun capture the imagination. The 2.5 km long beach enjoys the added benefit of the warm Gulf Stream.

Sweden

Gotland, Götaland
(above)

The Swedish island of Gotland lies northwest of the island of Öland in the Baltic Sea. Due to its mild climate, the island is a popular holiday destination. It is made chiefly of limestone. Among things worth seeing on Gotland are the "sea-stacks", limestone pillars up to 10 m high that stand on the rocky beaches at Digerhuvud and Langhammars.

Stora Nassa, Stockholm
(below)

Stora Nassa is the most well-known island group in the skerry landscape just outside of Stockholm. The little islands are typical features of Swedish, Norwegian, and Finnish landscapes. They were sculpted by ice sheets and can be as large as several square kilometres. They often have vegetation and the occasional small house, as here in Stora Nassa.

Finland

Rauma, Western Finland
(lower left)

The offshore islands and wide sand dunes on the outskirts of this coastal city in Southwestern Finland make quite an impression. But Rauma is famous for its sixteenth and seventeenth century wooden houses, which form the historical heart of the city. Anyone who visits the beautifully preserved city centre can also try regional fish specialities at the marketplace.

Ireland

Achill Island, Connaught
(upper right)

Achill Island lies off the west coast of Ireland and its raw beauty is legendary. Visitors can climb the still untouched, inaccessible Cliffs of Croaghaun or drive to Keem Beach. Tucked between hills, the country's most beautiful beach is a favourite meeting place for surfers.

Inch, Kerry
(upper RH page)

The Dingle Peninsula is a marvellous place for long walks in a pristine natural setting. There is a beautiful, 6 km long beach at Inch. You should especially see it at low tide when light reflects off a thin layer of sea water onto the sand. The ruins of Minard Castle are also on the Dingle Peninsula.

Great Britain

Newquay, Cornwall
(upper left/LH page)

Newquay on Cornwall's southwest coast prides itself on being England's "surf city", and international surfing contests are held on Fistral Beach and other area beaches. This former fishing village offers a total of eleven sandy beaches that stretch for over 10 km all together, such that everyone may find his or her own personal favourite.

Seilebost Beach, Isle of Harris
(below)

The islands of Lewis and Harris are part of the Outer Hebrides, which lie off the west coast of Scotland. They are really two halves of a single island; but since they are divided a mountain chain, they are considered separate islands. On Harris you'll find the wildest landscapes in the Hebrides and one of the loveliest beaches in Scotland, Seilebost Beach on Tarbert Bay.

Durdle Door, Dorset
(above)

A natural limestone arch called the Durdle Door is a gateway for wind and sea. It lies on the Isle of Purbeck, which is not an island at all. But the name dates back to a time when it could only be reached via a single route with an expensive toll. The lovely scenery consists of gentle hills and heather, chalk cliffs and golden sandy beaches.

Brighton, East Sussex
(below)

Brighton is one of the UK's largest, most popular coastal cities. You can reach it in less than an hour by train from London. This is seen as a distinct advantage by residents of the capital city, and the same can be said of many foreign tourists. The famous Brighton Pier dates back to 1899: it boasts an amusement park, a restaurant, and all sorts of arcades.

L'Ancresse Bay, Guernsey
(above)

Guernsey is the second largest of Britain's Channel Islands. L'Ancresse Common, a superb area with many sand dunes, lies on the north side of the island in Vale Parish. You'll find several very beautiful beaches here, all of which are surrounded by sand dunes. Some are in sheltered little bays like Port Soif, but there are also much larger beaches like the one at L'Ancresse Bay.

Portelet Bay, Jersey
(below)

The largest of the Channel Islands, Jersey, is also the sunniest island in all of Great Britain. The mild climate and broad beaches attract lots of holidaymakers. Beautiful Portelet Bay lies in St. Brelade Parish on the island's southwest coast. The beach is only accessible via a long staircase that leads from the cliffs to the beach.

Belgium

Oostduinkerke, West Flanders
(below)

Shell collectors and sand castle sculptors get their money's worth in Oostduinkerke. The seaside resort is also famous for its unusual tradition of fisherman on horseback, a practice that continues to fascinate visitors to this day. Standing in the surf with reed baskets on their backs, the draught horses slowly reel in nets filled with shrimps and prawns.

The Netherlands

Schiermonnikoog National Park
(upper left)

Schiermonnikoog is the smallest of five, inhabited Dutch Frisian Islands. Its name means "island of the grey monks", for it was once owned by the monks of Klaarkamp Abbey. The island is now a popular holiday destination that prides itself on having one of Europe's broadest bathing beaches. The beach is actually up to 1 km wide in several places! The eastern half of the island is a national park and bird sanctuary.

De Koog, Texel
(upper right)

Texel is the largest of the West Frisian Islands. This is where "all of Holland" can be found "on a single island". The scenery is exceptionally diverse: The open sea roars in along the west coast, and this is where you'll find long sandy beaches with dunes all around them. The east coast is calmer and borders on the Wadden Sea. The island's tourist centre, De Koog, lies on the northwest coast.

Zandvoort, North Holland
(above)

The town of Zandvoort boasts one of the most famous beach resorts in the Netherlands. The 9 km long beach is Zandvoort's biggest attraction and has plenty of room for sailing, surfing and beach volleyball. There are forty-one beach pavilions that offer culinary delights and seats that are sheltered from the wind. Flying over the beach is a Blue Flag, the voluntary eco-label for a clean, safe beach.

Scheveningen, The Hague
(below)

Scheveningen is a sub district of The Hague and lies about 6 km from the city centre. Originally a little fishing village, it is now the largest seaside resort in the Netherlands. The 381 m long pier has an observation tower, and you'll get a marvellous view of the North See from there. The shops, cafes and restaurants on the promenade are an open invitation to stroll.

Denmark

Rømø, Southern Denmark
(above)

Rømø is Denmark's southernmost North Sea Island and lies just about 5 km north of Sylt. Since Rømø has the widest beach in Europe, it can rightly claim special status! At low tide, it is about 2.5 km wide and 8.5 km long. And it has the neighbouring island of Sylt to thank for such a spacious beach, because sand carried away from Sylt washes ashore again on Rømø.

Jutland *(below)*

Lying between the North and Baltic Seas, Denmark's Jutland Peninsula is a much-frequented holiday destination. That's because of its grassy coastal dunes, as well as the mild climate brought about by the Gulf Stream. Given the spacious beaches, everyone will find a spot along the coastline where he or she can be alone with nature.

Ærø, Southern Denmark (above)

Little villages lined up like pearls on a necklace make the elongated island of Ærø one of the loveliest in the Danish South Sea Islands. Surrounded by Schleswig-Holstein and the islands of Funen and Langeland, this isle with a mild climate lies in the middle of a prime sailing area. Its hilly landscapes, secluded beaches and steep cliffs also attract many hikers.

Løkken, North Jutland (below)

Hallmarks of the wide, 10 km long beach at Løkken in Northwest Denmark include little white bathhouses and permission to drive your car right up to the water. Holiday guests who spend the afternoon in the dunes can watch as fishing boats are dragged onto the beach, and they can stock up on freshly caught fish right there.

Germany

Møn, Zealand
(upper left)

Fine sand beaches, green forests and wonderfully blue water are what make the island of Møn a real gem among Denmark's South Sea Islands. The famous white limestone Cliffs of Møn form a 6 km long, up to 120 m high coastline in the eastern part of the island. Their German counterpart lies farther south on the Baltic Sea island of Rügen.

Dueodde, Bornholm
(lower left)

The Danish Baltic Sea island of Bornholm is known for its diverse landscapes and mild climate. Visitors may choose between rocky coastlines, picturesque seaports and wide sandy beaches. Due to its white sands and exceptionally clean water, Dueodde Beach is way up on the list of favourites among holidaymakers.

Juist
(lower RH page)

Juist is an East Frisian pearl of the sea. The 17 km long beach that stretches around the entire island makes it especially popular. Here and there, bright spots of colour in the fine sand bear witness to the lively beach life. There are beach chairs, tents and people doing beach callisthenics on this traffic-free island. But you'll also find quiet, solitary little spots.

Spiekeroog
(above)

One side of the green island of Spiekeroog has black pines and groves of poplars with owls and falcons living in them; on the other side, you'll find dunes, beaches and the North Sea. And there's not a single car in between - just pedestrians and bike riders. That's because Spiekeroog is a traffic-free zone without exhaust fumes or engine noise.

Borkum *(above)*

The days when pirates sought safe harbour on Borkum is long past. Today the largest of the seven East Frisian Islands is a refuge for holidaymakers. They come to the isle to take extended walks along the beach, to watch sea gulls gliding in the wind, and to sweep across the dunes on horseback.

Langeoog *(centre)*

A 14 km long beach and fabulous sand hills are Langeoog's calling cards. The most famous landmark on this North Sea island is the water tower, and you'll get the best view of the up to 20 m high dunes from there. Day trippers to the island can also watch seals from an observation platform.

St. Peter-Ording, Schleswig-Holstein *(below)*

Germany's largest seaside resort is a veritable Eldorado for kite and wind surfers. The boundlessly long, wide beach provides plenty of room for turning manoeuvres. Other visitors come to St. Peter-Ording to boat around the Wadden Sea or to cool down in the sea at high tide. You'll get a fantastic view of the sea from the stilt houses on the beach.

Heligoland *(above)*

Day trippers are the main visitors to this North Sea island. Jutting out of the sea in the northwestern part is a 47 m high red sandstone rock known as "Tall Anna": it is the symbol of Heligoland and the island's main attraction. Overnight guests can ferry over to the nearby isle of Düne and watch seals romping on the beach.

Norderney *(below)*

Time seems to stand still on the 15 km long, 2.5 km wide North Sea island of Norderney. The stress of daily life rolls off travellers the minute they set foot on this East Frisian island. And it's no wonder, given the seemingly endless beaches, dunes and tidal flats. Their thoughts turn to the fresh air, stiff breezes and tidal cycles.

Westerland, Sylt *(below)*

Westerland is the main town on the island of Sylt and the hub for excursions to points north and south. Every visitor to Westerland's 40 km long beach will surely find an empty beach chair. With so many options for wind surfing, surf boarding and kite boarding, this extensive beach is a paradise for water sports lovers.

Red Cliffs, Sylt *(RH page)*

Between Wennigstedt and Kampen, you'll find the famous Red Cliffs and a steep, 30 m high coastline with beautiful dune land-scapes, fine sandy beaches, and a little light-house. This stretch of beach in the western part of Sylt faces the sea, so when the sun goes down and the towering rocks are bathed in red light, the view is absolutely stunning.

Fehmarn *(above)*

One of the sunniest spots in Germany lies at the back of the Fehmarn Sound Bridge on the North Sea island of the same name. With 1,920 hours of sun per year, it also sports lagoons, spits and impressive dune land-scapes. The remarkable diving areas around Fehmarn are also a big draw. You can explore a total of seventeen shipwrecks from war-ships to trawlers.

Timmendorf Beach, Schleswig-Holstein *(centre)*

Timmendorf Beach is a chic seaside resort in Lübeck Bay. Holidaymakers can relax on the 8 km long beach, take a day trip to the Brodten Cliffs, or go on a diving trip to see shipwrecks in the North Sea. Visitors to the Sea Life Centre can learn about the maritime world without ever getting their feet wet.

Travemünde, Schleswig-Holstein *(upper right)*

Situated in Lübeck Bay, Travemünde Beach is a great place to watch ocean liners passing by. The sandy beach extends along the bay for 3 km. This elegant resort at the mouth of the Trave is a popular sailing area. Anyone who longs for peace and seclusion can make his or her way to the cliffs that start beyond Travemünde near Brodten.

Prerow, Mecklenburg-Western Pomerania *(upper left)*

You may go into raptures at the sight of Prerow's spacious sandy beach, white sands, softly sloping shoreline, and azure water. The north beach is famous for its longstanding tradition of nudist bathing, which continues along several sections to this day. The primeval Darße Forest to the west of the bathing beach is also worth seeing.

Kühlungsborn, Mecklenburg-Western Pomerania *(below)*

The seaside resort of Kühlungsborn lies on the North Sea Coast of Mecklenburg. Visitors who end here come mainly on account of the long boardwalk with an unobscured view of the sea, as well as the lovingly restored villas and guest houses. Other attractions that merit a quick trip include the pier and the wharf at the boat harbour.

Binz, Rügen *(above)*

The largest seaside resort on the island of Rügen lies on a bay that is flanked by forests of the Schmale Heide (EN: narrow moorland) and the reedy banks of the Schmachter See. The fine sand, magnificent beach villas along the promenade, the mild, refreshing climate, and nearly 2,000 hours of annual sunshine make Binz an attractive destination for those who love the water.

Hiddensee *(below)*

This traffic-free island lies west of Rügen and is reachable by water taxi from Stralsund or Rügen. You're headed for tranquillity on Hiddensee. Island guests may have a look at the cliffs and lighthouse on the north coast, watch the screeching gulls while strolling in the dunes, or go hunting for shells on one of the solitary beaches.

Poland

Ahlbeck, Usedom
(above)

The seaside resort of Ahlbeck lies directly on the border with Poland. This resort on the island of Usedom was once the easternmost *Kaiserbad* (EN: imperial spa), and the pier attests to its historical past. Each year, energetic swimmers and spectators gather at Ahlbeck Beach on Valentine's Day to ring in the season with an ice bath. In the summer months, lots of people go to Ahlbeck for a seaside holiday.

Wannsee, Berlin
(below)

A kilometer long, 50 m wide bathing beach lies on the eastern shore of the Greater Wannsee. Inland waters bring the sand here from the North Sea. As the hit song says, the moment the first rays of sun warm the Berlin air, people pack their bathing trunks, head directly to Wannsee, and stake out a spot on the beach.

Niechorze, Western Pomerania
(upper RH page)

Niechorze is a Polish beach resort on the North Sea. It's quite close to the Liwia Luza Lagoon. Anyone who is athletically inclined should tackle the 200 lighthouse steps on the forested waterside cliffs, as the view of the beach, its three jetties and wooden breakwater is absolutely fantastic from up there. On a clear day, you can even spot the Danish island of Bornholm 85 km away.

Hungary

Tihany, Lake Balaton
(below)

The Tihany Peninsula, the town of Tihany, and several beautiful bathing options are located on the north shore of Lake Balaton. The peninsula divides the lake into northern and southern sections. Rich in flora and fauna, it was declared Hungary's first nature reserve in 1952. Although a party atmosphere dominates some areas of Lake Balaton, you won't notice any of the hustle and bustle here. There are also two crater lakes on the peninsula.

Lithuania

Curonian Spit *(above)*

Situated between Klaipeda and Lesnoje, the Curonian Spit is a 98 km long strip of land with beaches on it. It belongs partly to Lithuania, partly to Russia, and consists entirely of sand. In the past, the vast shifting dunes have buried entire towns, but there are plants growing on them nowadays. They are also a UNESCO World Heritage Site.

Curonian Lagoon *(lower RH page)*

The Curonian Lagoon is part of the North Sea. It belongs to Lithuania and Russia, and gets its name from the tribe known as Kurs or Curonians. The most beautiful beaches on the Baltic Sea lie on its banks. The lagoon is fed by several estuaries of the Neman River, and the Curonian Spit separates it from the open sea. There is a sound at the northern end of the Curonian Spit, and they call it the "Memel Deep".

Latvia

Jurmala *(lower LH page)*

Jurmala is a lively seaside resort in the Gulf of Riga. It lies where the Lielupe River flows into the Baltic Sea and is chiefly known for its white sandy beach that stretches for many kilometres. Its curative mineral springs are another reason why Jurmala has become a popular spa resort. Numerous healing and wellness options continue to attract more and more holidaymakers.

Livonia *(above)*

Holidaymakers will find pristine landscapes along the 100 km long Baltic Sea coast between Riga and the Estonian border. In lieu of holiday resorts with big hotels, you'll find deserted beaches, and that goes for the summer months as well. The rocky coastline is also famous for its picturesque fishing villages, dune landscapes and salt marshes.

Estonia

Pärnu *(above)*

The seaport of Pärnu is the most important resort on the Estonian coast. Its 3 km long beach and modern promenade lie on Pärnu Bay, a northern inlet of the Gulf of Riga. Since the water is shallow, Pärnu has become an especially popular holiday destination for families with children. Estonia's summer capital also has a yacht harbour that is well worth seeing.

Võsu, Lahemaa National Park *(below)*

Lahemaa National Park lies east of Tallinn. This natural paradise has pine forests, moors, bogs, lakes, rivers, beautiful bays, and beaches that jut out into the Gulf of Finland. The Võsu seaside resort is surrounded by forests: its beach and picturesque pensions are charming spots for those in search of rest and relaxation.

Russia

Sochi, Southern Russia *(above)*

Wholesome mountain air, fresh sea breezes, and the subtropical climate draw holiday-makers to this spa and seaside resort in the region of Krasnodar Krai on the Black Sea coast. The same can be said of its mineral springs and spacious beach promenade. In fashionable Sochi on the Russian Riviera, you can also go water skiing and boating or take an underwater tour.

Barguzinsky Bay, Lake Baikal *(below)*

Reaching depths of up to 1,637 m, Lake Baikal is the deepest freshwater lake in the world. The lake is 728 km long and 48 km wide on average. Surrounded by high mountains, it contains even more water than the Baltic Sea. UNESCO declared it a World Heritage Site in 1996. Several national parks, including the Barguzinsky Nature Reserve, are located on its banks.

Portugal

Cascais, Estremadura
(above)

You'll find many sandy coves along the very rocky coast of Costa do Estoril, and one of them is near Cascais. The town used to be a fishing village, but is now geared toward holidaymakers. *Boca do Inferno* (EN: Hell's Mouth), located 2 km away on the coastal road to Guincho, is well worth seeing. The "Almighty Din" is a huge cauldron that the sea has carved into the rocks, and it causes the waves to effervesce.

Buarcos, Coimbra
(centre)

The holiday paradise of Buarcos lies on the Costa de Prata between Lisbon and Porto. Long sandy beaches, rough Atlantic waters, and windy conditions make the area popular with surfers and bathers who enjoy plunging into the waves. For inexperienced swimmers and families with children, however, there are many days that call for caution when entering the water.

Ponta da Piedade, The Algarve
(upper RH page)

The promontory known as *Ponta da Piedade* is south of Lagos in the Algarve. Its high cliffs jut way out into the sea. You'll be captivated by the cliffs and fantastic grotto landscapes with bizarre rock formations, tunnels and arches. The best way to explore the grottoes is by boat. In the summertime, fishing boat excursions are available from Lagos to the grottoes.

Praia de Amoreira, The Algarve
(lower LH page)

The Praia de Amoreira about 3 km north of Aljezur is a picture perfect beach. This beautiful, spacious beach in the Algarve borders on an area of sand dunes; it's not overcrowded and access to the water is level, such that even less experienced swimmers can go in without worrying. The waves are somewhat higher further out and thus attract a lot of windsurfers.

Zavial, The Algarve
(below)

There is a gorgeous beach not far from the town of Zavial in the Algarve. Lying between Lagos and Sagres, this undeveloped inlet is not only popular with those who take seaside holidays; it also attracts numerous surfers who enjoy plunging into the fantastically surging Atlantic waves. And a much frequented beach bar sees to it that culinary delights are readily available.

Praia do Camilo, The Algarve
(above)

Halfway between Lagos and the Ponta da Piedade headway, a 195 step staircase leads down to the Praia do Camilo. Situated beneath high cliffs, this beach is among the most dramatic in the Algarve. The Atlantic waves flood the beach at high tide, leaving very little open space on the sand. A tunnel through the rocks leads to the neighbouring cove.

Praia do Três Irmãos,
The Algarve *(centre)*

Three huge boulders are the reason it's called "Three Brothers' Beach". The beach begins around 1.5 km southeast of Alvor. There are fields of dunes at the back of the beach, but you'll also find plenty of fish restaurants in between. Anyone looking for solitude should retire to the western edge of the beach. It can only be reached on foot, and that's why not many people visit it.

Praia da Rocha, The Algarve
(below)

The rocks at Praia da Rocha are favourite motifs for picture postcards. A century ago, this chic seaside resort in the Algarve was still the province of the ultra wealthy. These days, the powdery wide sandy beach is a popular tourist destination with numerous amenities, including a promenade, beach stalls, a multitude of large hotels, plus entertaining leisure and sports activities for every imaginable taste.

Praia Dona Ana, The Algarve
(above)

Praia Dona Ana is Lagos' main day trip destination. The approximately 200 m long beach lies beneath sandstone cliffs, and overhanging rock formations divide it into two sections. You get to the beach via a trail that runs along the cliffs in a southerly direction from Praia de Pinhão.

Prainha, The Algarve
(below)

A beautiful beach with impressive rock formations lies in the immediate vicinity of the Algarve's secret capital, Portimão. Sun worshippers and bathers alike get their money's worth at diminutive Prainha Beach. Beach access is a bit unusual: taking the lift is the best way to get down the steep cliffs.

Benagil, The Algarve
(above)

The little Algarve fishing village of Benagil lies between Armação de Pêra and Portimão. The paved coastal road leads straight down into the narrow seaside inlet, so it gets very congested in the summertime. The unusual rock formations are striking. A very lovely footpath goes over the cliffs to the neighbouring beach of Praia da Marinha.

Praia Sao Rafael, The Algarve
(below)

Praia Sao Rafael, an unspoilt beach with spectacular rock formations, lies 4 km west of the tourist centre, Albufeira. The S. Rafael rocks are also called "libraries". Various, perpendicular layers of rock tilt upward from the waterline and look like books stacked on a shelf. It's best to view them from a boat.

Praia da Marinha, The Algarve
(above)

Praia da Marinha was chosen Portuguese Beach of the Year in 1998. It's easy for anyone who sees its golden sands and imposing cliffs to understand why it received this distinction. And yet the beach is not overly crowded. When the water reaches a certain level, conical rocks divide the beach in two. But extremely high tides render it inaccessible.

Albufeira, The Algarve
(below)

A wide selection of sandy beaches with blue-green water, picturesque inlets, and pine groves surrounds the former fishing village of Albufeira. And the beaches go on for kilometres. Narrow, winding lanes lead directly downhill from the picture perfect old town to the beach, which is lined with restaurants and taverns that will serve you grilled sardines, a local delicacy.

Praia da Falésia, The Algarve
(lower left)

Praia da Falésia is the most beautiful beach in the Algarve, and a glance at the colourful rock formations reveals why that is so. The luminous, colourfully striped white sandstone rocks are impressive and provide popular subject matter for photographers. Time and again, this undeveloped stretch of coastline will catch you by surprise with scenic highlights such as these.

Caniçal, Madeira
(lower right)

The town of Caniçal on the eastern part of Madeira Island usually creates bit of a sleepy impression. The only sandy beach on the eastern end of the island is found here, and its dark sand is striking. But to get there, you have to make a steep descent into the bay. History buffs can visit the Whale Museum in Caniçal. The museum provides an historical overview of whaling in Madeira.

Porto Santo
(above)

The island of Porto Santo lies 50 km east of Madeira. The island has a mountainous interior. A sandy beach stretches for over 9 km along the southern coast. The extremely fine, light coloured sand earned Porto Santo the nickname, "Golden Island". The sand purportedly has an analgesic effect on rheumatism and arthritis. This healing property has yet to be scientifically proven, however.

Spain

Playa de las Catedrales, Costa de Lugo *(above)*

The Galician municipality of Ribadeo lies on the border with the neighbouring autonomous community of Asturias. There are several very beautiful, yet sparsely visited sandy beaches to the west of the city. The most spectacular and famous one is Playa de las Cathedrales, which gets its name from a number of strangely hollowed out rocks formations. But you can only view them at ebb tide, as the sea covers them when the tide is up.

Playa Cuevas del Mar, Costa Verde *(below)*

A coastal landscape called the Costa Verde (EN: verdant coast) skirts the Bay of Biscay in northern Spain. One of the loveliest beaches in the land sits between Llanes and Ribadasella. The fascinating golden sand, turquoise sea and matchless rock formations of Playa Cuevas del Mar make unforgettable photographic motifs.

Tossa de Mar, Costa Brava
(above)

The Catalonian seaside resort of Tossa de Mar lies between cliffs that drop steeply into the sea. The historic streets of the old town are enclosed by medieval walls with fortified towers. Beyond Tossa de Mar, the scenic road to Sant Feliu de Guíxols offers panoramas of strange rocky landscapes and picturesque golden beaches.

Llanfranc, Costa Brava
(below)

Llanfranc lies on the Costa Brava, a stretch of coastline along the Spanish Mediterranean in the autonomous community of Catalonia. In this fishing village, holidaymakers find golden sand and beautiful seas. The wild landscape of Cap de Begur is right nearby. Numerous beaches in this area have been awarded the Blue Flag.

Lloret de Mar, Costa Brava
(above)

During the summer months, the holiday resort of Lloret de Mar on the Costa Brava is a much frequented playground for young people from all over Europe. In addition to sea, sun and sand, there are plenty of choices including a promenade, discotheques and pubs. Sporting options range from diving to paragliding and water skiing.

Sant Pol de Mar, Costa del Maresme *(centre)*

Regardless of whether one is looking for action or leisure, everyone gets his money's worth in Sant Pol de Mar. A person can peacefully sunbathe on the city's marvellous beaches, which are located between Canet de Mar and Calella about 50 km from Barcelona. Anyone who prefers sport can indulge in numerous types of water sports.

Benidorm, Costa Blanca
(below)

Benidorm has the most skyscrapers per square metre of any city but Manhattan. High-rises of the major hotel chains dominate the skyline of this city in the Valencia Region. As a resort town, Benidorm can look back on a long tradition: Francisco Ronda opened the first swimming bath at Platja de Levant in 1893. Along with Playa de Poniente, 2.5 km long Platja de Levant is the city's most important beach.

Marbella, Costa del Sol
(above)

The holiday resort of Marbella is a fabulous combination of beaches, mountains, sun and nightlife in a year round temperate climate. In addition to sandy beaches along a 26 km coastline, this seaside resort in southern Spain provides guests with several yacht harbours, luxury hotels, golf courses, well-kept boulevards, parks and public gardens. And there are leisure activities to suit every taste.

Tarifa, Costa de la Luz
(centre)

Tarifa in the Andalusian province of Cádiz is the southernmost municipality on the European mainland. Nowhere are Europe and Africa closer, because the Strait of Gibraltar that separates the two continents is only 14 km wide here. Yet Tarifa is famous for more than its geographical location: the exceptional wind conditions have made the town a dream destination for windsurfers.

Cala Galdana, Menorca
(below)

Cala Galdana lies south of Ferrieres on the southern coast of Menorca. It was one of the first coves on the island to be set up as a holiday resort. Although the tourist market is now fully developed, the beauty of the place remains unaffected. A sheltered beach lies between the cliffs on the eastern side of the cove, while steep rocks tower above the western portion.

Binibèquer, Menorca *(above)*

Minorca, the northernmost of the Balearic Islands, has a multitude of beaches and coves. Binibèquer lies on the southern coast, south of the island's capital, Maó (Port Mahon). It's the most popular beach in the area below Sant Lluís. A long karstic promontory protects the almost completely undeveloped beach, so the deep-blue water is always calm and exquisitely clear.

Cap de Formentor, Majorca *(below)*

The largest island in the Balearic group has always been extremely popular with European holidaymakers, and rightly so: Majorca has splendid beaches on offer with wonderfully shallow water, including Cap de Formentor in the extreme northeast. Moreover, fascinating underwater areas along the rugged coastline of the Formentor Peninsula are full of corky sea fingers and encrusting stick anemones.

Alcúdia, Majorca
(above)

The Bay of Alcúdia lies in the northern part of one of Europe's favourite holiday islands. It is an important commercial and tourist centre. The white sandy beach extends for more than 25 km along the bay. Time and again, you'll find secluded spots without a trace of mass tourism. The mountains are also relatively close, so many hikers choose the Bay of Alcúdia as their point of departure.

Cala Mondragó, Majorca
(centre)

The lovely inlets of Cala Mondragó stretch out along the southern coast of Majorca to the south of Cala d'Or. A footpath connects the twin beaches, which get a lot of traffic in the high season. The bay is a protected area, as well as the starting point of a hiking trail that takes you to the fishing harbour of Cala Figueira in around an hour.

Andraitx, Majorca
(below)

In Platja Sant Elm, the coastal resort of Puerto Andraitx has an exquisite, spacious sandy beach on offer. The island of Sa Dragonera lies just off the coast, and there are two reasons why it's name is entirely appropriate. On the one hand, this uninhabited rocky island is shaped like a recumbent dragon; on the other hand, a unique species of lizard, the Lilford's Wall Lizard, lives in the Sa Dragonera Nature Reserve.

Cala Salada, Ibiza *(above)*

The protected sandy cove of Cala Salada near Sant Antonio may still be a hot tip. Surrounded by hills and pine forests, its white sands and clear, turquoise-blue water are especially picturesque. A stone tower stands on a rocky promontory at the right side of the cove. From there, a path leads to another little cove with a narrow beach.

Playa d'en Bossa, Ibiza *(below)*

Playa d'en Bossa is one of Ibiza's best known beaches, but fame does not make it any less beautiful. The gently sloping, kilometre long sandy beach begins just 4 km beyond the capital, Cuitat d'Eivissa. Sun worshippers and water sports enthusiasts are drawn here in equal measure. And the capital has a whole host of discotheques, shops and bars that give everyone something to do in the evening.

Playa Francesca, La Graciosa
(above)

The 28 square km island of La Graciosa lies north of Lanzarote in the Canary Islands. It has been part of the Chinijo Marine Reserve since 1986. A 172 m high volcanic hill, Montaña Amarilla, is located in the southwestern part of the island. At its foot sits Playa Francesa, a small, but excellent swimming beach where sand is continually interspersed with rocks.

Playa de Ses Illetes, Formentera
(below)

The 82 km² island of Formentera is only about 20 km south of Ibiza in the Balearic Islands. Playa de Ses Illetes is a gorgeous beach on a sparsely populated tongue of land in the north of the island near Es Pujols: its clear water and light coloured sand will surely draw you in. Fully aware of its special qualities, many holidaymakers to the neighbouring island of Ibiza travel over by boat.

El Golfo, Lanzarote *(above)*

Located in the southwestern part of Lanzarote, the little village of El Golfo is particularly famous for its excellent fish restaurants. But one of the best-known sights on the entire island, a remarkable lagoon, lies a bit farther south. The lagoon has formed in a sunken volcanic crater, part of which lies in the sea; its striking green colour comes from wigeongrass (Rupia maritima).

Playa Blanca, Lanzarote *(below)*

Playa Blanca was once a peaceful fishing village, but is now among the most important tourist centres on Lanzarote's southern coast. The 194 m high Montaña Roja volcano lies west of town. But the northeastern part of the island has several small beaches no longer than 100 to 400 metres, and volcanic rocks form a barrier between them. Built in 1936, the Faro de Pechiguera lighthouse is another popular spot among photographers.

Playas de Papagayo, Lanzarote
(above)

There is no doubt that the best beaches on Lanzarote lie in the south: this is where you'll find brightly coloured beaches nestled in rocky coves with blue-green water lapping all around. At Playas de Papagayo, you can leave your cares behind, cool off in the sea from time to time, or take a closer look at the marine flora and fauna. Just don a snorkel, mask and flippers, and off you go!

Playa de Sotavento, Fuerteventura *(lower left)*

The snow-white sands and wonderfully blue water of Playa de Sotavento are near the holiday resort of Costa Calma. Playa de Sotavento is part of an extensive, 30 km long beach, and no matter how many holidaymakers flock to the area, you can still find secluded spots. The landscape around the beaches is extremely diverse: from mud flats to gigantic shifting dunes, you'll discover nature in all its variety.

Morro Jable, Fuerteventura
(lower right)

Morro Jable is Fuenteventura's most important holiday resort. Situated on the Jandía Peninsula, it lies in a valley between two rocky hillsides that face the Atlantic. The Jandía Playa hotel complex starts here and stretches for several kilometres along the marvellous sandy beach.

Playa de Corralejo, Fuerteventura (above)

Playa de Corralejo is near Fuenteventura's northernmost municipality of La Oliva, which was a notorious den of pirates and smugglers in the seventeenth century. But today's holidaymakers are wooed here by its beautiful beach. The mostly rocky sea floor makes the water look especially clear. A large area of dunes lies immediately south of the beach.

Costa Calma, Fuerteventura (below)

The popular holiday resort of Costa Calma lies on the Jandía Peninsula in the southern part of Fuerteventura. The first hotels set up shop here in the 1970s: businesses and restaurants soon followed. Holidaymakers particularly love the brightly coloured, fine sand beach: due to its optimal wind conditions, windsurfing championships are frequently held here.

Maspalomas, Gran Canaria
(below)

Maspalomas is a resort town at the southern tip of Gran Canaria with sandy beaches that stretch for several kilometres. The sand is made of finely ground sea shells. Its dune landscapes are just the right spot for a Jeep safari. When the wind sweeps away your tracks in an instant and forms wavy lines in the idyllic, sandy wilderness, the breathtaking beauty of this place becomes apparent.

Playa del Inglés, Gran Canaria
(upper right)

The people of this district in the municipality of San Bartolomé de Tirajana had very specific holidaymakers in mind, and so they called it the "Beach of the English". Although they originally targeted English tourists, holidaymakers from all over the world now come to this 13 km long beach in the southeast coast of Gran Canaria. The shallow water and gently sloping beach make it especially popular among families with children.

Playa de las Teresitas, Tenerife
(lower right)

Playa de las Teresitas near San Andrés is the island's flagship beach. Four million bags of Sahara sand were heaped onto it in 1973. The resulting golden colour is unusual for a volcanic island like Tenerife. An offshore barrier keeps high waves from crashing onto the beach. The village has retained its historic charm, but you won't find many hotels here.

Playa de la Arena, Tenerife
(upper LH page)

Tenerife is the largest of the Canary Islands. Playa de la Arena belongs to the municipality of Santiago del Teide in the western part of Tenerife. It's a new little tourist town: many Brits and Germans have second homes there. Playa de la Arena is famous for its black beaches and shallow seas.

Playa de las Americas, Tenerife
(centre)

You can still spot the unspoilt black coastline of this volcanic island at Playa de las Americas in the southwestern part of Tenerife. They have actually tried to pile sand onto the beach, but such attempts were always thwarted by heavy seas. Nevertheless, Las Americas draws large numbers of sun worshippers by day and is the centre of nightlife on Tenerife.

Valle Gran Rey, La Gomera
(above)

The "Valley of the Great King" on the island of La Gomera gets its name from Hupalupa. He was the leader of the Guanches, the original inhabitants of the Canary Islands. The landscapes in this valley may strike you as somewhat exotic. There are banana plantations and palm trees with little houses popping up in between. Lots of hippies settled in the valley in the 1970's, and many of them were from Germany.

Playa del Verodal, El Hierro
(RH page)

El Hierro is the smallest of the seven big volcanic islands in the Canaries. It was declared a UNESCO Biosphere Reserve in 2000. Since it doesn't have any "classic" beaches, the island has been spared from mass tourism. Nevertheless, the red Playa del Verodal on the west coast is well worth seeing. Due to the high waves, however, only experienced swimmers should dare to go in the water.

Puerto Naos, La Palma
(below)

La Palma is the northwesternmost of the seven big Canary Islands and, like most of its neighbours, is of volcanic origin. This island in the Atlantic has thus far been spared from mass tourism, but has an outstanding beach in the village of Puerto Naos. Puerto Naos Beach was awarded the Blue Flag of the European Union, which is only given to those that meet the highest standards.

France

Mont-Saint-Michel Bay, Manche (above)

Mont-Saint-Michel and its Benedictine abbey are well-known postcard motifs. At high tide, the island is surrounded by water and can only be reached via a raised causeway. The bay stretches from Canale to Granville, and you can take a marvellous stroll in the mud flats. But considering the enormous 15 m tidal range, extreme caution is advised.

Étretat, Seine-Maritime (lower left)

The main attractions in Étretat are crags, washed-out chalk cliffs and beaches. Differences between low and high tide cause them to change form as practically nowhere else on Earth. The rocky arch to the west of the seaside resort is a very special eye catcher and resembles an elephant's trunk. At low tide, visitors have access to the adjoining beach via a tunnel that's been blasted out of the rock.

Saint-Malo, Ille-et-Vilaine (lower right)

Any visit to Brittany simply must include the walled port city of Saint-Malo. As you tour the city wall, you can let your gaze wander along the narrow streets of the historic medieval fortress and out over the Atlantic. Just across from Saint-Malo is the seaside resort of Dinard, which has perfect conditions for kite boarding, catamaran sailing and windsurfing.

Crozon, Finistère
(above)

From moorlands and pine forests to sandy beaches flanked by craggy rock formations, the Crozon Peninsula in northwest Brittany prominently displays the wildness of nature. Visitors really ought to climb the steep cliffs at Pointe de Penhir, so as to enjoy the stunning view of the Atlantic Ocean and other capes on the Crozon Peninsula.

Cabourg, Calvados
(below)

In the nineteenth century, the Parisian upper classes often set themselves up at the seaside resort of Cabourg on the English Channel. Holidaymakers can still get a whiff of Belle Époque ambience or follow in the footsteps of the writer Marcel Proust, who stayed at the Grand Hotel. And all of this takes place against the backdrop of a lovely promenade, striped beach changing rooms, and elegant villas.

Saint Tugen, Finistère
(above)

In the summer months, surfers and families with children are the first to head for the western tip of Brittany to collect shells and indulge in water sports on the spacious sandy beach at Saint Tugen. The fishing harbour of Audierne is right nearby. Freshly caught fish and regional fish specialities are available at the town market.

Dune du Pyla, Gironde
(below)

It's 117 m high after all. So it's no wonder that Europe's largest sand dune offers a fantastic panoramic view of the Archachon Basin, the Atlantic Ocean, and the surrounding pine forests. Seaside visitors can watch paragliders and hang gliders, and enjoy local seafood specialities in the little restaurants on the promenade.

Biarritz, Pyrénées-Atlantiques
(lower RH page)

The waves at Grande Plage in Biarritz can easily match those in California. And that's why Europe's surfing capital has been nicknamed, "Home of the Surf". Holidaymakers who don't dare to get on a surfboard can stroll along the promenade to the lighthouse or explore the underwater grottoes.

Saint-Tropez, Côte d'Azur
(above)

The illustrious name of this little fishing village has epitomized jet-set tourism since the 1950s. Brigitte Bardot's film, *And God Created Woman*, made her world famous overnight, and the picturesque film location of Saint-Tropez along with her. As if by magic, this Mediterranean holiday resort has attracted up-and-coming stars and the general public ever since.

Menton, Côte d'Azur *(upper left)*

Menton is the easternmost city on the French Côte d'Azur. Shielded by the Maritime Alps, this Italianate seaside resort enjoys an especially mild climate. Lemon trees grow in the gardens. The city has an elegant promenade and lovely beach. In the old town, the pastel coloured houses and baroque cathedral are well worth seeing.

Cannes, Côte d'Azur *(lower left)*

The upscale shopping area on Boulevard de la Croisette lies right in the centre of Cannes. Stars from all over the world visit the boulevard once a year when the film festival gets going. But even when the festival isn't taking place, the palm-lined promenade, sandy beach and casinos of this chic seaside resort are meeting places for celebrities, as well as everyday people on holiday.

Nice, Côte d'Azur *(lower right)*

A once quiet coastal road in Nice was laid out as a fine promenade for eighteenth century English guests. Nowadays, life is really vibrant on the Promenade des Anglais: its luxury hotels, restaurants, palm trees, and flowery borders all exude fashionable glamour. Heads of state and celebrities stay in huge suites at the legendary Negresco Hotel.

Désert des Agriates, Corsica
(above)

The Désert des Agriates is a rocky desert on the island of Corsica near Saint-Florent. The place is fascinating, and its flora, called maquis, is decidedly typical of the Mediterranean. There are remote inlets and heavenly places along the ca. 35 km coastline. Day trippers can take a dip in the shimmering green water and enjoy these secluded spots all by themselves.

Palombaggia, Corsica
(below)

On the beach at Palombaggia travellers will find everything that's important for rest and relaxation. There are little beaches with craggy borders, pine forests, and boulders lying in the crystal clear water that bathers on holiday can rest on by the shore. The uninhabited Cerbicale Islands lie just off shore and are the perfect addition to this picture perfect setting.

Italy

Punta della Contessa, Elba
(above)

Laconella Beach lies on the southern part of the Mediterranean island of Elba in Tuscany. The beach is located in an enchanting cove with imposing cliffs that frame it: on one side is the Punta della Contessa headland, and Capo della Stella is on the other. If the skies are clear, you can see the silhouette of the island of Montecristo from the beach.

Lido di Jesolo, The Veneto
(below)

The Italian seaside resort of Jesolo is just a stone's throw from Venice. It's a great choice for anyone who wishes to combine a beach holiday with a visit to the Lagoon City. In Italy's second largest resort town, holiday-makers can cruise around the lagoon in a rented boat or immerse themselves in a good book on the golden beach.

Marina di Alberese, Tuscany
(upper RH page)

Marina di Alberese is an unspoilt sandy beach on the edge of the Maremma, a nature reserve in southern Tuscany. Maremma horses and cattle, as well as wild boars, wildcats and porcupines inhabit an area with characteristic maquis, pine forests, inland lakes, swamps, and little dunes.

Rimini, Emilia-Romagna
(lower left/RH page)

Since the 1950s, Germans have seen Rimini as the ultimate Italian holiday experience. And this resort on the Adriatic still draws a significant number of enthusiastic holiday-makers. The gently sloping, wide sandy beaches are particularly appealing for families with children. The Paganello, an international ultimate frisbee tournament, also takes place on the beach around Eastertime.

Baia delle Zagare, Apulia
(lower right)

The Gargano Peninsula in Apulia juts out into the Adriatic for about 50 km. Tremendous cliffs, rocky plateaus and grottoes make this an attractive area for nature lovers. Baia delle Zagare is surrounded by pine forests, olive groves and vineyards, and offers numerous leisure time activities for wind surfers and divers.

Positano, Campania
(LH page)

Characteristically steep lanes and staircases explain why the seaside resort of Positano is the Amalfi Coast's main attraction. White and rose coloured houses with impressive roof domes go all the way up the cliff. Lush bougainvilleas, as well as lemon and orange trees grow in the narrow gardens. Down on the beach you'll find spaghetti with mussels, and the sunsets are heavenly.

Capri, Campania
(lower left)

The Blue Grotto and the Faraglioni are the most interesting sights on this illustrious island. Faraglioni is the collective name given to three, porous stacks lying just off shore. The town of Capri and its chic shops are very trendy. You get to town by taking the funicular from the harbour. But this "pearl in the Gulf of Naples" also has quiet spots like the bay of Marina Piccola.

Tropea, Calabria
(lower right)

A sandstone cliff rises above the beach at Tropea, a medieval city on the Mediterranean coast of Calabria. The pilgrimage church of Santa Maria dell'Isola sits triumphantly atop the cliff. Visitors really should tackle the arduous path to the top, because they'll be rewarded with a spectacular view of Tropea, the surrounding mountains and deserted bays.

Capo Vaticano, Calabria
(above)

Capo Vaticano in southern Italy is simply filled with pristine natural wonders. All along this stretch of land are picturesque inlets with crystal clear water and rocky plateaus with spectacular panoramic views of the countryside. The underwater world is also very colourful. But the crowning touch to every day is watching the sun set over the Aeolian Islands.

Lipari, Aeolian Islands
(lower left)

A boat ride around the Aeolian Islands is simply a must, because you can explore little coves, crags, and delightful snorkelling spots that are otherwise inaccessible. On the north coast of this volcanic island you'll find spectacular pumice plateaus and Spiaggia Bianca, a beach that seems to meld into the turquoise blue sea.

Giardini Naxos, Sicily
(lower right)

The holiday paradise called Giardini Naxos (EN: Gardens of Naxos) get its name from the fact that it was the first Greek colony to be established on Sicily. Visitors can still visit the ancient ruins. People travel to Giardini Naxos and eastern Sicily for the beautiful sandy beaches, the promenade, and the wide range of hotels to choose from.

Cefalù, Sicily
(above)

This romantic city on Sicily's northern coast is one of the island's liveliest seaside resorts. A spectacular rock (IT: La Rocca) towers above Cefalù, and you'll discover the remains of a Temple of Diana atop it. Founded by the Phoenicians, the little town is also famous for its Norman style cathedral whose walls are decorated with Byzantine mosaics.

Lampedusa, Pelagic Islands
(lower left)

The island of Lampedusa lies between Tunisia and Sicily; its climate is quasi-African. Little Isola dei Conigli (EN: Rabbit Island) lies off Lampedusa's southern coast. Many visitors are attracted to the island because loggerhead turtles lay their eggs in the nature reserve each spring. The fine sand, white limestone rocks, and turquoise blue sea form a magically beautiful backdrop for this annual event.

Spiaggia del Principe, Sardinia
(lower right)

Spiaggia del Principe lies on Sardinia's Costa Smeralda (EN: Emerald Coast). The beach gets its name from Prince Karim Aga Khan IV, who bought up this ravishingly beautiful strip of coastline and was especially fond of this beach. The beach and rocks shimmer in shades of pink, such that holidaymakers see everything through rose-coloured glasses.

Bari Sardo, Sardinia
(above)

There is a rich array of heavenly holiday spots around Bari Sardo on the eastern coast of Sardinia. And since they can only be reached via rough trails, they are largely deserted. You'll get a view of the entire bay from Torre di Bari, and the tower's viewing platform provides an unobstructed view of the gulf.

Is Arutas, Sardinia
(upper left)

Is Arutas Beach has a pale rosy-white lustre that comes from tiny grains of quartz sand. The beach lies on the Sinis Peninsula in western Sardinia. This thinly settled area, its numerous lagoons, typical Sardinian shrubbery, craggy granite rocks, and cormorant colonies are an absolute paradise for anyone looking for rest and relaxation.

Porto Campana, Sardinia
(upper right)

The enormous sand dunes at Porto Campana Beach in southern Sardinia are particularly alluring. Beautiful beaches, crystal clear water, and favourable wind conditions explain why the area around Chia has become a playground for kite boarders and wind surfers. Beachgoers also like to watch these athletes performing jumps in the water.

Chia, Sardinia
(below)

Visitors take a scenic road to the Bay of Chia, where they arrive at a lagoon with an endlessly wide sandy beach and shimmering, turquoise and green water. Sun worshippers can often spot dolphins jumping in the inland lakes, which are inhabited by flamingos. You should also plan to see the ruins of the Phoenician city of Bithia.

Malta

Ramla Bay, Gozo (above)

A gorgeous beach lies on the north coast of the Mediterranean island of Gozo. The beach has thus far been spared from mass tourism. Ramla Bay lies between two rocky bluffs; its red sandy beach is a rare, but absolutely beautiful sight. This is the right spot for anyone who wishes to swim and sun bathe in calm surroundings.

Golden Bay, Malta (below)

Golden Bay, whose Maltese name is *Ir-Ramla tal-Mixquqa*, lies in the southwestern part of the Mediterranean island of Malta. Even though its beautiful beach is among the most popular on the island, it has remained a truly heavenly spot. A path along the coastline takes you to the neighbouring bays of Ghajn Tuffieha and Gnejna, both of which are somewhat more peaceful.

Croatia

Brač, Split-Dalmatia
(above)

Golden Horn lies on the Adriatic island of Brač and is considered the most beautiful beach in Croatia. It juts out into the sea for some 100 m and gets its name from its unique shape, which resembles a horn or crescent. The beach consists of little round pebbles. The current gradually moves them around, such that the tip of the horn sometimes points in one direction, sometimes in the other.

Donja Brela, Split-Dalmatia
(centre)

The town of Donja Brela likes to be referred to as "the pearl of the Dalmatian Riviera". And this popular tourist spot actually does have several picturesque pebble beaches lined with pine trees. Punta Rata Beach was even selected by *Forbes Magazine* as one of the ten most beautiful beaches in the world. Several, famous springs also bubble up beneath the surface of the sea.

Murter, Šibenik-Knin
(below)

The Adriatic island of Murter lies in the northwestern part of the Šibenik Archipelago. A bridge connects it to the city of Tisno. Most of the beaches on Murter are rocky, which gives the turquoise water a wonderfully clear appearance. The southwestern portion of the island consists mainly of steep, rocky walls with many sandy coves in between.

Dubrovnik, Dubrovnik-Neretva
(RH page)

Dubrovnik is a beautiful jewel of the south Croatian coast. It is a particularly special treasure, thanks to its medieval lanes, walkable city wall (just under 2 km long), and location on a rocky plateau with the sea lapping all around. Visitors to Dubrovnik's Banje Beach have a marvellous view of the old city which, by the way, is completely off limits to traffic.

Greece

Lassi, Kefalonia (above)

Due to its proximity to the island's main city, Argostoli, the beach resort of Lassi is a favourite holiday destination. Kefalonia is the largest of the Ionian Islands. Another of Kefalonia's main attractions, the subterranean lake in Melisani Cave, lies on the opposite coast. Rays of sunshine come through the partially collapsed limestone roof, causing the water to glow deep blue.

Paleokastritsa, Corfu (below)

Surrounded by olive groves and cypresses, the dreamy resort of Paleokastrista on the northwest coast of Corfu is an idyllic spot with numerous cliffs and white pebble beaches. Some of the smaller coves cannot be reached by land. Boats carry holidaymakers to invitingly secluded beaches where they can snorkel and swim in the clear water.

Navagio, Zakynthos
(upper left)

A path on the northwest coast of Akynthos leads to a spot in the cliffs with a stunning view. Visitors gasp with delight when they see the deep blue water at Navagio Bay and Shipwreck Beach. This southernmost island in the Ionians is also a paradise for divers, who come across rocky underwater arches, ravines, grotto landscapes, and sea turtles.

Elafonisos, The Peloponnese
(upper right)

Desert-like beaches and glassy seas are typical features of this little islet that lies between The Peloponnese and Cythira. Depending on the depth of the water, the sea sparkles in shades of azure and light blue. Elafonisos has several beaches, but the Simos Lagoon with its two beaches is the most beautiful: that's because of its crystal clear water and the view of the neighbouring island from this location.

Balos, Crete
(below)

The lagoon beach of Balos has fine, white sand made from seashells. It lies on the northwest side of the Gramvousa Peninsula on the island of Crete. This remote, idyllic beach can only be reached by water or via a path with a stone staircase. Excursion boats stop at the quiet inlet, but are mainly headed for the offshore island of Imeri Gramvousa.

Matala, Crete *(centre)*

This former fishing village has become a thriving holiday spot. Caves in the sandstone cliffs are Mattala's main attraction. This is where Christians found refuge in ancient times and hippies like Bob Dylan, Joni Mitchell and Cat Stevens would later hunker down from time to time. There are gorgeous beaches in the surrounding area.

Sarakiniko, Milos *(above)*

Bizarre rock formations, hot springs, thermal baths, and whitewashed cliff houses make the Cycladic Island of Milos uniquely beautiful. Sarakiniko's white pumice rock formations give it a lunar appearance. They surround the tiny beach and reach up into the radiant blue sky.

Mykonos, The Cyclades *(below)*

White houses, famous windmills, and golden beaches with wonderfully clear water set the island of Mynonos in the Cyclades apart. The most beautiful stretches of beach are in the south, because this part of the island is sheltered from the wind. Kalafati is a great place for underwater touring. Divers can sight schools of barracuda and dragonheads.

Agia Anna, Amorgos *(above)*

Jagged Amorgos in the Cyclades Islands has spectacular coastal cliffs that drop straight into the sea for up to 800 m. The white monastery of Panagia Chozovoitissa is one of the island's main attractions. It walls hug the 180 m high cliffs. The beach at Agia Anna has the best bathing and snorkelling on the island.

Faliraki, Rhodes *(below)*

The former fishing village of Faliraki is now one of Rhodes' most important holiday resorts. It offers countless recreational opportunities, such as sailing, surfing and waterskiing. Idyllic Vagies Bay is just 3 km away. It was given to Anthony Quinn as a gift following his depiction of Alexis Zorba in the highly successful movie, *Zorba, the Greek.*

Lalaria, Skiathos *(upper left)*

Skiathos in the Sporades Islands is blessed with gorgeous beaches. A seaside destination for discriminating tastes, its picturesque villages and green hilly landscapes are what make it a jewel of the Greek Islands. Boat tours to the Bay of Lalaria begin at the Skiathos town harbour. Lalaria Beach is a heavenly spot with grottoes, rocks and crystal clear water.

Sithonia, Chalkidiki *(upper right)*

Sithonia is the third digit of the Chalkidiki Peninsula, which is shaped like a hand. On this tongue of land in the Aegean, visitors will encounter striking mountain ranges, overgrown slopes, idyllic coves, and long sandy beaches with shady pines. There are numerous cliffs, and anyone who visits Sani Beach will be able to enjoy an impressive view of Mount Athos.

Kira Panagia, Karpathos *(below)*

The craggy, mountainous island of Karpathos in the southern Dodecaneses is beautifully wild. Lots of wind surfers visit it because of the favourable wind conditions. This holiday paradise has steep coastlines with caves and magical sandy coves. Kira Panagia on the eastern coast is a picture perfect beach, and a lovely church with a red cupola perches regally above it.

Bulgaria

Bolata, Dobrudja *(above)*

The romantic Bay of Bolata is situated on the northern coast of the Black Sea; it lies in a nature reserve that is home to many rare plant and animal species. Its golden sandy beach has an impressive border of shimmering reddish rocks. Visitors who decide to take a boat tour have an excellent chance of spotting seal colonies and dolphins in the lovely clean water.

Sinemorets, Burgas *(below)*

What makes Sinemorets so alluring is the combination of green beech forests, sandy beaches in various, radiant golden hues, rock formations, and its location at the mouth the Veleka River. The village lies on a peninsula along the southern coast of the Black Sea and is precisely the right place for nature lovers seeking an absolutely tranquil holiday.

Romania

Mamaia *(above)*

A suburb of Constanta, Mamaia is Romania's most important Black Sea resort. It lies on a 7 km long, 300 m wide tongue of land between the Black Sea and Siutghiol, a fresh water lake. It gets very crowded here in the summertime. Countless numbers of sun worshippers take over the fine white sands of its narrow beach.

Constanta *(below)*

Constanta is Romania's major Black Sea harbour, an important link between Europe and Asia. So many goods change hands here that the city has been nicknamed, "Rotterdam of the East". There are several beautiful seaside resorts in the vicinity. Constanta even has a beach of its own, Plage Modern, which lies in the city centre.

Turkey

Bodrum, Mugla *(upper left)*

Bodrum was built on the spot where the ancient city of Halikarnassos once stood. The Mausoleum of Halikarnassos was among the Seven Wonders of the World. Today this holiday resort has several vibrant beaches. You can still find remains of the ancient city lying between Bodrum's many little white houses. A well preserved, fifteenth century Crusader fortress also lies at the front of the harbour.

Marmaris, Mugla *(upper right)*

The coastal city of Marmaris lies on the Bozburun Peninsula in the Turkish Aegean. The name means "three hanged architects": a sultan had and fortress built and was not happy with it, so he angrily ordered the architects to be put to death. But this gruesome past is nowhere to be found at beautiful Icemeler Beach, a pebble beach that lies 8 km west of the city.

Blue Lagoon, Oludeniz *(below)*

It won't take you long to see why the Blue Lagoon near Oludeniz is Turkey's most frequently photographed beach. The white sandy beach lies in a bay with crystal clear water. And it's especially picturesque at sunset. The Blue Lagoon is not as deserted as one might like; but regardless of all the hustle and bustle, it's still a gem.

Cleopatra Beach, Alanya
(above)

An Egyptian queen once swam here. Marcus Antonius apparently gave the city of Alanya to Cleopatra as a wedding gift, and the two spent their honeymoon in the gentle waves of the Turkish Riviera. A multitude of holidaymakers now follows suit and comes here on holiday. People amuse themselves with modern sport, such as diving, sailing and surfing.

Kaputas, Antalya
(below)

A dreamy beach just 150 m long is tucked into the steep cliffs at Antalya, which lies on the coastal road between Kas and Kalkan. It comes as no surprise that the turquoise-green cove with golden sand gets really busy in the summertime. But you can still enjoy the sun and sea at Kaputas Beach. And experienced swimmers can swim the 500 m stretch to the Blue Grotto.

Cypress

Famagusta *(above)*

Although the name, Famagusta, means "hidden in the sand", this popular holiday resort has no reason to hide. In addition to beautiful beaches, holidaymakers will also find a historic-cultural monument. The Citadel and Othello's Tower lie in the harbour. Events apparently took place in this tower that inspired Shakespeare to write his famous play.

Golden Sands *(lower left)*

People claim that the most beautiful beach on the island of Cypress is located in the north on the way to the famous Apostolos Andreas Monastery. The golden sands stretch for several kilometres along the coast, attracting sun worshippers and swimmers with their beauty. A peninsula juts into the sea at the western end of the beach. That's where you will find the remains of old cisterns and another swimming cove.

Asterias Beach *(lower right)*

Asterias Beach (EN: Starfish Beach) was the first beach on Cypress to be awarded the Blue Flag. It lies on Macronissos Bay, which is about 4 km from the popular holiday resort of Ayia Napa on the southern coast of Cypress. Its white sands and clear water look just like something out of a picture book. The beach is surrounded by pine trees.

ASIA

DELIGHTFULLY DIVERSE CONTRASTS

Asia, the largest continent on Earth, stretches across a wealth of attractive landscapes and coastal areas from Siberia in the Far North to the Equator in the South. The countries of the Near East and Arabia evoke memories of *One Thousand and One Nights.* In Dubai or Abu Dhabi, you will thus find ultra-modern luxury hotels and air-conditioned shopping centres surrounded by fascinating desert landscapes. Countless small and larger islands of Indonesia, Malaysia, Thailand, and the Philippines compete to see who has the loveliest beach of all. The Maldives probably have ultimate coastal landscapes. Their atolls offer dreamy, snow-white beaches and turquoise lagoons that invite you to relax. This island state also has much to offer below the surface of the water. Diver's hearts will surely leap for joy at the thought of Sipadan's underwater world, which shimmers in every imaginable colour. Further to the north, you'll be fascinated by the singularly beautiful landscapes of the Caspian Sea, Lake Yssykköl in Kyrgyzstan, and the Aral Sea in Kazakhstan. Asia is a continent of many contrasts whose diverse peoples and landscapes have one thing in common: they continue to impress, visit after visit.

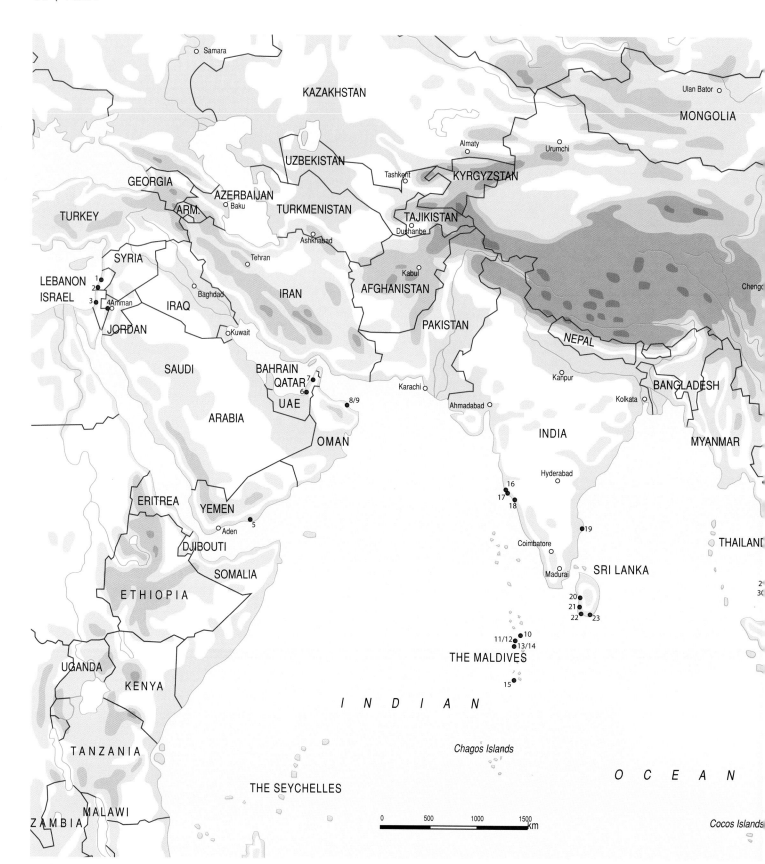

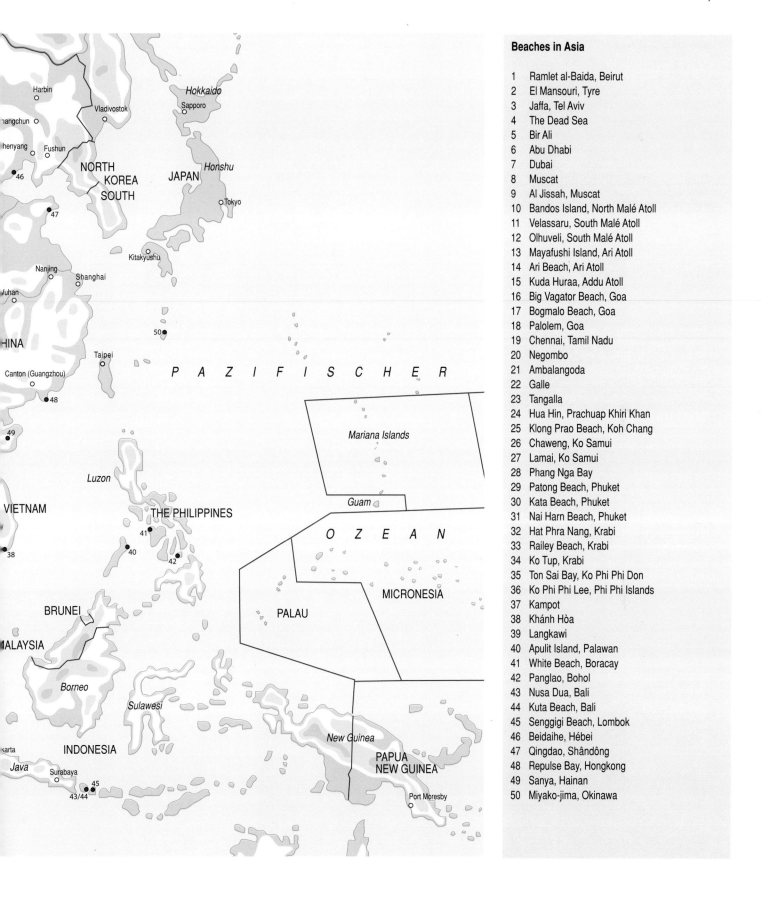

Beaches in Asia

1   Ramlet al-Baida, Beirut
2   El Mansouri, Tyre
3   Jaffa, Tel Aviv
4   The Dead Sea
5   Bir Ali
6   Abu Dhabi
7   Dubai
8   Muscat
9   Al Jissah, Muscat
10 Bandos Island, North Malé Atoll
11 Velassaru, South Malé Atoll
12 Olhuveli, South Malé Atoll
13 Mayafushi Island, Ari Atoll
14 Ari Beach, Ari Atoll
15 Kuda Huraa, Addu Atoll
16 Big Vagator Beach, Goa
17 Bogmalo Beach, Goa
18 Palolem, Goa
19 Chennai, Tamil Nadu
20 Negombo
21 Ambalangoda
22 Galle
23 Tangalla
24 Hua Hin, Prachuap Khiri Khan
25 Klong Prao Beach, Koh Chang
26 Chaweng, Ko Samui
27 Lamai, Ko Samui
28 Phang Nga Bay
29 Patong Beach, Phuket
30 Kata Beach, Phuket
31 Nai Harn Beach, Phuket
32 Hat Phra Nang, Krabi
33 Railey Beach, Krabi
34 Ko Tup, Krabi
35 Ton Sai Bay, Ko Phi Phi Don
36 Ko Phi Phi Lee, Phi Phi Islands
37 Kampot
38 Khánh Hòa
39 Langkawi
40 Apulit Island, Palawan
41 White Beach, Boracay
42 Panglao, Bohol
43 Nusa Dua, Bali
44 Kuta Beach, Bali
45 Senggigi Beach, Lombok
46 Beidaihe, Hébei
47 Qingdao, Shândông
48 Repulse Bay, Hongkong
49 Sanya, Hainan
50 Miyako-jima, Okinawa

Lebanon

Ramlet al Baida, Beirut *(above)*

Ramlet al baida means "white sand" in Arabic, and that's exactly what you'll find on this 1.6 km long beach along the Mediterranean. But this is just one of the scenic highlights you'll encounter in and around Beirut. The Lebanese capital lies along a narrow coastal strip, and the hinterlands are mountainous. Sunsets here are picturesque.

El Mansouri, Tyre *(below)*

El Mansouri is known above all for its sea-turtles, which come onto the beach to lay their eggs. This Mediterranean coastline is part of Tyre, an ancient Phoenician seaport that is now Lebanon's fourth largest city. Due to the great number of historic places in Tyre, it has been entered on the list of UNESCO World Heritage Sites.

Israel

The Dead Sea *(above)*

This sea is "dead" because no plant or animal can live in it. This is due to its salt content, which can be as high as 33%. But this has clear advantages for non-swimmers, who can bathe safely here: the salt water will keep them afloat, and it's not possible to sink below the surface. Favourite seaside resorts, some of which lie just 30 km from Jerusalem, include Enot Zukim near Qumran, En Gedi, Neve Zohar, and En Boqeq.

Jaffa, Tel Aviv *(below)*

The ancient seaport of Jaffa lies south of Tel Aviv on the Mediterranean. It has an impressively colourful mix of Jewish, Christian, and Muslim inhabitants. You can see this in the architecture as well, for it has everything from ancient buildings to ultra-modern skyscrapers. In the summer months, Jaffa's beach admittedly draws locals, but lots of holidaymakers have discovered it as well.

United Arab Emirates

Yemen

Dubai *(upper left)*

In recent years, Dubai has become a booming tourist destination. About one-fourth of the emirate's income stems from the tourist trade. In addition to glorious beaches and man-made islands in the Persian Gulf, holidaymakers will also find numerous spectacular buildings. One of them is the Burj al Arab Hotel, whose enterprising features include a helicopter landing pad and underwater restaurant.

Abu Dhabi *(below)*

Abu Dhabi is the richest city on Earth. This emirate had no more than 4,000 residents before oil was discovered here in 1958; over 1.8 million people from 120 countries now live in Abu Dhabi. This city lies on a T-shaped peninsula in the Persian Gulf and two, multilane bridges link it to the mainland. Its contemporary architecture and broad, sandy beaches offer great views at all times of day.

Bir Ali *(upper right)*

The Bible mentions the port of Qana on the Arabian Sea, and the modern city of Bir Ali lies in that very spot. In ancient times, the harbour played an important role in the incense trade. You can still visit the ruins today. This fishing village with its fine, white sandy beach and turquoise-blue water is surrounded by shifting dunes, a jagged volcanic crater, and towering cliffs.

Oman

Muscat (above)

The capital of the Sultanate of Oman is remarkably green. Two Portuguese forts, as well as numerous mercantile buildings and mansions, testify to its long history as a commercial harbour. A lovely walking path on the coastal road to Mutrah leads along the Kalbooh Peninsula to begin with. The Gulf of Oman comes into view on the western side, and lots of little rocks also tower out of the sea at this point.

Al Jissah, Muscat (below)

The 500 m long, private beach in the Bay of Al Jissah is famous for its pristine sand, and its turtle breeding ground is also very popular. Green and hawksbill turtles come on land here to lay their eggs. But no harm must come to them in the process. And that's why the government of Oman has appointed "turtle guardians" to keep a watchful eye on these rare, sea dwelling creatures.

The Maldives

Bandos Island, North Malé Atoll *(above)*

The circular island of Bandos is one of the liveliest and best-known in the Maldives, and is therefore included in many tour packages. This island has everything a true island paradise needs: a white, sandy beach, rich array of palm trees, manicured tropical gardens and, needless to say, a lagoon with crystal clear water.

Velassaru, South Malé Atoll *(lower left)*

The island of Velassaru lies on the northwestern edge of the South Malé Atoll. More recently, it goes by the name of Laguna Beach. The name derives from its unusually large lagoon, which can reach depths of up to 18 m. Since it lacks a reef of its own, however, the diving and snorkelling conditions are not ideal. But you can bask in the fabulous sunshine on its wide, sandy beach, which more than makes up for this drawback.

Olhuveli, South Malé Atoll *(lower right)*

Olhuveli is one of the more upscale and expensive of the islands in the South Malé Atoll. This lush isle lies in the southern part, and its long sandbar juts out into the sea. There is a large lagoon in the western portion of the island that's just perfect for bathing and all kinds of water sports. A long bridge over the east lagoon leads directly to the reef, which lies between 100 to 150 m off shore.

Mayafushi Island, Ari Atoll
(above)

Tourist accommodations on Mayafushi Island in the North Ari Atoll are among the finest in the area, and it's easy to understand why they chose this particular island for development. You'll be captivated by the snow-white sandy beaches on all sides, as well as the tropical vegetation and heavenly lagoon, which is perfectly suited to bathing.

Ari Beach, Ari Atoll
(lower left)

From kayaking and jet skiing to windsurfing and catamaran sailing, superb Ari Beach on Ari Atoll offers excellent opportunities for all manner of water sport. The lagoon on this island has very little coral, which makes it perfect for bathing. Anyone needing a bit of exercise can circle this elongated island in about an hour.

Kuda Huraa, Addu Atoll
(lower right)

If you come to Kuda Huraa Island off the Addu Atoll, you can be sure of one thing: this island is absolutely exclusive, for it belongs to a luxury hotel chain. Whoever can afford it will most definitely get pampered here. A flawless, sandy beach encircles the island, and one of the most lovely bathing lagoons in all of the Maldives lies at the western side of the island.

India

Bogmalo Beach, Goa
(above)

Bogmalo Beach is one of the most beautiful in the State of Goa. It is situated about 7 km from the city of Vasco da Gama. Goa's largest city got its name from the famous Portuguese explorer, who was the first European to set foot in India (1498). Goa was a Portuguese enclave for centuries and was not annexed by India until 1961.

Big Vagator Beach, Goa
(lower LH page)

Big Vagator Beach lies along the 100 km long coastline to the north of Panaji, the capital of the Indian State of Goa. Rising above the golden sands and shining blue water of the Arabian Sea, Chapara Fort provides a most impressive setting for this heavenly beach. And anyone who finds the chaos excessive can retreat to one of the little, nearby coves.

Palolem, Goa
(upper right)

In 2004, the beginning sequence of *The Bourne Conspiracy* with Matt Damon was filmed on the beach at Palolem, and movie buffs may well recognize it for this reason. But Hollywood is not alone: many tourists also love this 2 km stretch of beach. They come here to enjoy the unspoilt natural setting and shallow water that's great for swimming.

Chennai, Tamil Nadu
(lower right)

Chennai was known as Madras until 1996. The country's fourth largest city lies in the Gulf of Bengal on India's southeast coast. The capital of the State of Tamil Nadu has several truly beautiful beaches, among them the 13 km long Marina Beach. You'll find statues of famous Indians on the street side of this sandy beach. And so Mahatma Gandhi is among those who watch over beach guests.

Sri Lanka

Galle *(above)*

Galle (pronounced "Gaul") lies on the south-west point of this island state. In addition to broad stretches of beach, it has the largest preserved European fortress in Asia. Built by the Portuguese in 1588, the Dutch enlarged it in the seventeenth century, and the rampart is truly impressive. The old city centre and fort are now a UNESCO World Heritage Site.

Negombo *(below)*

Negombo lies 30 km north of the capital, Colombo. Located at the edge of the Negombo Lagoon, the city now has about 65,000 residents. This little seaport lives almost exclusively from fishing and tourism. In contrast to other Sri Lankan tourist areas, holidaymakers will find relatively quiet beaches with fine sand. The diving and windsurfing are also fantastic.

Tangalla *(above)*

You'll find several of the loveliest beaches in the land near Tangalla, a city approximately 190 km south of Colombo. With lush vegetation and gorgeous palm trees, this beach is the embodiment of a secluded, tropical paradise. And the magical ambience of sunsets over the Indian Ocean is not to be missed.

Ambalangoda *(below)*

The 35,000 residents of Ambalangoda suffered heavy losses in the tsunami of Christmas 2004. But the people and coastline are slowly recovering from this natural disaster. The sandy beach with rocky outcroppings and palm trees remains a true feast for the eyes. Ambalangoda is a centre of traditional Sri Lankan mask making.

Thailand

Hua Hin, Prachuap Khiri Khan
(upper left)

The country's oldest seaside resort lies in the Gulf of Thailand. Not only does it attract foreign visitors; the Thais themselves treasure this seaside resort, and even the royal family has a summer residence here. The city beach and its rocky outcroppings stretch for 6 km. Hau Hin's favourable location protects it from bad weather, especially during the rainy season, which means that the season runs all year long.

Klong Prao Beach, Koh Chang
(below)

Koh Chang means "elephant island", and its contours really do resemble an elephant's head. It is also Thailand's second largest island. Anyone looking for relaxation should seek out the beach at Klong Prao. This fine white sand beach is 4 km long, and the estuary of the Klong Prao River divides it in two.

Phang Nga Bay
(above)

Impressive limestone rocks and turquoise-blue water provide an artistic backdrop for this world famous bay in southern Thailand. Movie fans will recognize one rocky pinnacle in particular, because it gets blown up in the James Bond film, *The Man with the Golden Gun.* This was a great special effect, because you can still find this awesome rock in Phang Nga Bay today.

Chaweng, Ko Samui
(upper right/LH page)

Ko Samui is the country's third largest island and one of its favourite holiday destinations. Its sandy beaches stretch for a total of 26 km. One of them, Chaweng, lies on the island's eastern coast. Although Chaweng is one of the most frequented beaches on the island, its wide sandy beach, lush coconut palms and clear, warm salt water are still a glorious sight.

Lamai, Ko Samui
(below)

Lamai Beach on the eastern coast of Ko Sumui Island is not as crowded as the better known Chaweng. There are certainly many hotels and bungalow communities. But holidaymakers seem to spread out quite nicely along the 4 km long, crescent shaped bay fringed with overhanging coconut palms. A coral reef lies off the eastern part of the beach and keeps high waves away from the shore.

Nai Harn Beach, Phuket (above)

Nai Harn Beach on the southern tip of Phuket is just one of the island's many dreamy beaches. And it offers a peaceful alternative. The fine, white sand beach and picturesque lagoon are bordered on both side by rocky hills and have coconut palms growing on them in some spots. Romantic sunsets from the nearby vantage point of Laem Prom Thep are best enjoyed with a partner.

Patong Beach, Phuket (below)

Patong is the most popular beach on Thailand's holiday island of Phuket. It has a well developed tourism infrastructure, including numerous diving schools that offer excursions to nearby diving areas. Koh Dok Mai, a 30 m high rock face, and Shark Point are not far from Patong. And you can watch leopard sharks from the safety of three large rock formations at Shark Point.

Kata Beach, Phuket *(above)*

Kata Beach lies on two bays along the southwest coast of Phuket: Kata Noi is relatively quiet, while Kata Yai is just as beautiful, but somewhat noisier. A rocky ledge separates the two bays, and you'll get a glorious view of the beaches and ocean from there. If you like to snorkel, you should make your way to the north end, where you'll find several rocks and the little island of Ko Pu.

Hat Phra Nang, Krabi *(below)*

There is a series of beautiful beaches near the little town of Krabi, but you can only reach them by boat. One of them, Hat Phra Nang Beach, has white sand and offshore rock towers that make it very picturesque. Even though it has just one luxurious hotel complex, this heavenly beach is also open to non-paying visitors.

Ko Tup, Krabi
(above)

A group of little, uninhabited islands lies between Phuket and Krabi. One of them is tiny Ko Tup, which is connected to neighbouring Chicken Island by a sandbar. The fantastic beaches on these islands are mainly filled with day trippers. But there are several beautiful coral reefs that snorkelers can also explore.

Railey Beach, Krabi
(below)

There is a little peninsula between the city of Krabi and popular Ao Nang Beach. And since limestone rocks block the land route, you can only access it by boat. You'll be charmed by the quiet, relaxed atmosphere of mythically archaic Railey Beach, which lies on the peninsula.

Cambodia

Ton Sai Bay, Ko Phi Phi Don
(lower left)
Ko Phi Phi Don belongs to the Phi Phi Islands and actually consists of two islands which are connected by a narrow strip of land. This is how its truly beautiful double bay came about: Ton Sai Bay lies on one side, Lo Dalam Bay on the other. You'll get a fantastic view of these two bays by climbing up to the island's lookout point. But be prepared to work up a sweat in the process.

Ko Phi Phi Lee, Phi Phi Islands
(above)
In *The Beach,* Leonardo DiCaprio is searching for the classic beach and lands on the tiny island of Ko Phi Phi Lee in Maya Bay. When Alex Garland made a movie version of the book, the beach became a veritable legend. But along with fame came lots of environmental polluters, so the island was declared a national park, and visitors must now pay a fee to get in.

Kampot
(lower right)
The peaceful city of Kampot lies just a few kilometres from the Gulf of Thailand. You can take a series of interesting day trips from here, e.g., to Bokor Hill National Park or nearby Kep. Kep was Cambodia's most important seaside resort in the 1970s, but its splendid villas were destroyed in the civil war. The glorious beach on Rabbit Island lies just offshore.

Vietnam

Khánh Hòa (above)

Along the 385 km coastline of Khánh Hòa Province are hundreds of islands with picturesque bays. One the most beautiful natural harbours in the world, Cam Ranh Bay, is among them. Several glorious beaches lies in the vicinity of this bay. American soldiers who were stationed here called it "Vietnam's Hawaii", and they were right!

Malaysia

Langkawi (centre)

Langkawi is an island that lies off the northwest coast of Malaysia in the archipelago of the same name. The archipelago sits directly on the border with Thailand. Its white beaches, lush rainforests and craggy mountain peaks were long considered Malaysia's best kept secret. But Langkawi and the island of Penang are now the most popular holiday spots in the country.

The Philippines

Apulit Island, Palawan
(above)

The Philippines are made up of 7,000 islands, so everyone will surely find their own personal dream island here. Would Apulit Island fit the bill? It's privately owned and belongs to El Nido Resorts. Holidaymakers can choose between sunning themselves on its white beach and swimming or snorkelling in the warm ocean.

White Beach, Boracay
(lower LH page)

Although a mere 7 km long, Boracay Island draws throngs of visitors each year. And White Beach is the reason they come here. This 3.5 km long beach is considered one of the most beautiful on Earth. You can see its fine white sand and turquoise-blue water on many a wall photo. Favourably situated on the downwind side of the island, White Beach has an ideal climate in the summer months.

Panglao, Bohol
(below)

The little island of Panglao lies just off the coast of Bohol and has some of the loveliest beaches in the country. Its sandy beaches are so white that they nearly blind you in the midday sun. In addition to fascinating beaches, Panglao also has a many different types of marine fauna. Around 250 species of crustaceans and 2,500 kinds of molluscs live in the surrounding waters.

Indonesia

Senggigi Beach, Lombok
(upper left)
Anyone looking to spend a classic beach holiday on Lombok should go directly to this 13 km stretch of coastline north of Ampenan. Holidaymakers will find luxury hotels, as well as inexpensive accommodations, plus fantastic beaches in solitary bays. You can even book excursions to nearby diving areas from here.

Kuta Beach, Bali
(upper RH page)
Balinese holidaymaking centres around the kilometre long stretch of sand at Kuta Beach, which is especially popular among Australians, Japanese and Europeans. It's like a magnet that draws them here to swim, surf, and get a tan. Numerous bars, restaurants and clubs see to it that nightlife gets going by day.

Nusa Dua, Bali
(below)

Nusa Dua lies on a peninsula in southern Bali. This is one of the nicest spots on the island, so it's hardly surprising that people have a good time here. The beaches are like powdered sugar, the water so clear that you can see to the very bottom. And with an outstanding selection of water sports that run the gamut from snorkelling and sailing to surfing, everyone will surely find something to suit their taste.

China

Beidaihe, Hebei *(above)*

Beidaihe is a district in the Eastern Chinese city of Qinhuangdao. To European visitors, it may look like a Chinese version of Rimini. And Beidaihe really does bear greater resemblance to a Western seaside resort than an Asian city. Yet not everyone can enjoy the 10 km long beach: only privileged functionaries of the Communist Party and affluent tourists have access to it.

Sanya, Hainan *(centre)*

Hainan Island on the south coast of China is often referred to as "Hawaii of the East". And little wonder: its white and golden hued beaches, deep blue sea, tropical rainforest, gentle hillsides, and average yearly temperatures of 25 °C practically invite comparison. The island's main seaside resort, Sanya, has a very well developed infrastructure. Lying in the south, its water remains at a balmy 28 °C year round.

Qingdao, Shandong *(below)*

Qingdao lies on the Shândông Peninsula in Eastern China and is one of the few larger Chinese seaside resorts. Its mild climate draws holidaymakers to swim or simply stroll on the beach year round. On account of its favorable winds, which also make it very popular with sailors, Qingdao was chosen to host the sailing events of the 2008 Olympic Games in Beijing.

Repulse Bay, Hongkong *(below)*

Repulse Bay lies in the southern part of Hongkong. This is the ideal sanctuary for all who wish to escape the overcrowded streets of the metropolis. The gentle wave patterns make this beach an excellent choice, even for inexperienced swimmers in whatever stage of life. Watching over the bathers are statues of Kwun Yum, the goddess of mercy and compassion, and Tin Hau, the patron saint of fishermen.

Japan

Miyakojima, Okinawa *(above)*

The Ryûkû island chain begins to the south of Japan's main islands, then subdivides into numerous archipelagos. Miyako is one of these island groups, and its blindingly white beaches are famous. The Ueno German Culture Village is a theme park with typical German buildings and furnishings that symbolize friendly German-Japanese relations.

AFRICA

AFRICA CASTS ITS MAGIC SPELL

Lonely beaches and bustling cities, impenetrable rain forests and broad savannahs, plus a multiplicity of cultures and peoples – the African Continent has all of these and much, much more. Even experienced divers go into raptures when they ponder the Red Sea's singular underwater world. And it doesn't matter whether they're venturing into a deep sea paradise like Dahab or travelling to the far less touristic beaches of Sudan. South Africa is the perfect combination of fascinating natural surroundings, wildlife exploration and relaxed beach culture, all of which takes place against the unforgettable backdrop of Table Mountain. But it's not just oceans and impressive coastlines that await you: rivers like the Congo or the Niger and lakes like Malawi or Victoria will captivate you with their superb scenery and rich animal life. And then, of course, there are the many islands: the Seychelles with their prominent granite rocks and snow white beaches, the honeymoon paradise of Mauritius, the Spice Islands of Zanzibar and La Réunion, which are a bit of France under the hot tropical sun. We'll bet that everyone will find their own personal island paradise here!

Beaches in Africa

1	Taghazout, Souss Massa National Park	6	Hammamet, Nabeul	15	Anse Intendance, Mahé	23	Saint Gilles, Saint-Paul	33	Ascension	41	Muizenberg, Western Cape

1   Taghazout,
    Souss Massa National
    Park
2   Agadir,
    Souss Massa National
    Park
3   Aglou,
    Souss Massa National
    Park
4   El Gzira,
    Souss Massa National
    Park
5   La Marsa, Tunis

6   Hammamet, Nabeul
7   Monastir, Nabeul
8   Sidi Mahrès, Djerba
9   Séguia, Djerba
10 Mombasa, Coast
    Province
11 Karera Beach,
    Bujumbura
12 Kiwengwa, Zanzibar
13 Jambiani Beach,
    Zanzibar
14 Benguerra,
    Bazaruto Archipelago

15 Anse Intendance,
    Mahé
16 Anse Lazio, Praslin
    Island
17 Ile Coco,
    The Seychelles
18 Anse Sévère, La Digue
19 Anse la Réunion,
    La Digue
20 Anse Source d'Argent,
    La Digue
21 Anse Cocos, La Digue
22 Petite-Île, Saint-Pierre

23 Saint Gilles, Saint-Paul
24 Boucan Canot,
    Saint-Paul
25 Flic en Flac, Black
    River
26 Ile aux Cerfs, Flacq
27 São Pedro, São
    Vicente
28 Santa Maria, Sal
29 Lumley
30 Abidjan
31 Pleasure Beach, Accra
32 São Tomé

33 Ascension
34 Cape Cross, Erongo
35 Walvis Bay, Erongo
36 Langebaan,
    Western Cape
37 Derde Steen,
    Western Cape
38 Bloubergstrand,
    Western Cape
39 Camps Bay,
    Western Cape
40 Sandy Bay,
    Western Cape

41 Muizenberg,
    Western Cape
42 Boulders Beach,
    Western Cape
43 Silversands Bay,
    Western Cape
44 Herolds Bay,
    Western Cape
45 Port Alfred, Eastern
    Cape
46 Durban,
    KwaZulu-Natal

Morocco

El Gzira, Souss Massa National Park *(above)*

El Gzira, also known as Legzira, lies in a completely secluded spot on the Atlantic coastline of Morocco between Sidi Ifni and Mirleft. You'll marvel at the stone gate on the offshore island. This impressive rock formation is also a popular photographic motif. As if that were not enough, this wild, romantic region is also very popular among anglers. Even swordfish are known to bite here.

Taghazout, Souss Massa National Park *(centre)*

The little romantic fishing village of Taghazout lies on the Atlantic about 20 km north of Agadir and gets a whopping 350 days of sunshine per year. But that's not all: its 10 km long sandy beach and several, neighbouring beaches ensure that you will really enjoy the sunshine. In the last few years, Taghazout has become a hot tip for surfers.

Aglou, Souss Massa National Park *(lower left)*

If you drive towards the Atlantic from Tiznit in southern Morocco, you'll arrive at the coastline near Aglou in about 20 km. This isolated beach will almost make you feel as if you had the entire coastline to yourself. Wide sandy beaches and gentle dunes alternate with steep cliffs, and the cliffs in turn stand proudly above the deep blue waters of the Atlantic Ocean.

Agadir, Souss Massa National Park *(lower right)*

The name Agadir means "fortified granary". This fishing harbour at the foot of the Atlas Mountains was founded by the Portuguese in 1505. Today, Agadir is a favourite holiday spot. Its big city appearance, wide streets, modern hotels, and European cafés may not seem particularly Moroccan. There are numerous wonderful beaches to discover here, among them beautiful Dix-sept and Imiouador.

Tunesia

La Marsa, Tunis *(below)*

La Marsa, the northernmost suburb of the capital, Tunis, has established itself as the summer residence of Tunisia's upper class. And you'll soon see why: the beach with its typical changing rooms is the perfect spot from which to view the pretty little white houses lined up along a gentle cliff in the midst of this verdant, forested community.

Hammamet, Nabeul *(above)*

Hammamet lies in the Gulf of Hammamet on the Mediterranean coast of northern Tunisia. This seaside resort can reflect on a long history: its kilometre long beaches have attracted tourists from all over the world since the beginning of the twentieth century. Hammamet is still the most popular seaside resort in the country, and the town's population quadruples in the summer months.

Monastir, Nabeul *(centre)*

Monastir lies about 160 km south of Tunis on the Gulf of Hammamet. Once a fishing port, this Mediterranean coastal city has become a favourite holiday spot with a fine, white sand beach and azure water. The cultural highlight of the area is the Ribat, one of Tunisia's most important, eighth century fortresses. Its beautifully preserved mosaics are a must see.

Sidi Mahrès, Djerba *(above)*

Djerba lies in the Gulf of Gabès off the east coast of Tunisia. It is the largest island in North Africa. European holidaymakers especially favour it as a travel destination. They greatly admire the island's flora, including prickly pears, palms, olive and pomegranate trees. And they certainly love its long sandy beaches, such as wide, shallow Sidi Mahrès on the south coast.

Séguia, Djerba *(below)*

Séguia Beach lies on the southern coast of Djerba between Cape Lalla Hardria and Aghir. This 5 km long beach is a true holiday paradise with numerous palm trees, fine white sand, and picturesque boulders in between. It's smaller and more tranquil than neighbouring Sidi Mahrès Beach. You can have the beach all to yourself, particularly if you go to the far end.

Kenya
Mombasa, Coast Province
(above)

Mombasa is Kenya's second largest city. It is situated on a 14 km² island bordered by two arms of the Indian Ocean. Mombasa is known for its heavenly beaches, which extend to the north and south of the city. Mombasa's Kilindini Harbour, the largest in the country, is a former river that was engulfed by rising seas. Since its channel cuts deeply into the coastline, they called it "Kilindini", which means "deep" in Swahili.

Burundi
Karera Beach, Bujumbura
(centre)

Not far from the capital city of Bujumbura, a broad, white strip of sand called Karera Beach spreads out at the northeast corner of Lake Tanganyika. It is the perfect spot to play beach volleyball or lie about in the lovely, cool shade. A restaurant caters to your culinary needs. Children can splash about in the shallow water. The nearest beach, Saga Beach, mainly attracts young people.

Tanzania
Kiwengwa, Zanzibar
(below)

Kiwenga, an autonomous region of Tanzania, lies on the east coast of Zanzibar. Since the snow white beaches and turquoise waters of the Indian Ocean provide the perfect setting for a dream holiday, an abundance of hotels and holiday facilities have sprung up here.
There are a number of offshore reefs that make it hard to swim at low tide. But the snorkelling is fabulous at high tide.

Jambiani Beach, Zanzibar
(below)

Zanzibar is one of the Spice Islands. The island's east coast is a bit more peaceful than the north. And Jambiani Beach, a picture perfect, fine sand beach, lies on the eastern shore. This beach has only one drawback: the water is extremely shallow, so you can only swim at high tide. There is also a little fishing village with lots of African ambience.

Mozambique

Benguerra, Bazaruto Archipelago *(above)*

Benguerra is an island in the Bazaruto Archipelago. If you wanted a short and sweet description, then "a tropical island paradise" would fit the bill. Benguerra lies 14 km off the coast in the warm waters of the Indian Ocean. Its brilliantly white sandy beaches, pristine natural setting, and outstanding diving areas lure countless holidaymakers. Among others things, you can scout out the dugong, a rare kind of manatee that is found in the surrounding coral reefs.

The Seychelles

Anse Lazio, Praslin *(above)*

Anse Lazio on Praslin Island, the second largest in the Seychelles, is undoubtedly one of the most beautiful beaches in the world. Perfectly formed Chevalier Bay has fine coral sand and is home to the coco-de-mer, a palm endemic to the Seychelles. This type of palm grows nowhere else. The Vallée de Mai Nature Reserve lies in the back country and provides a habitat for the Seychelles black parrot. It has been a World Heritage Site since 1983.

Anse Intendance, Mahé *(below)*

Anse Intendance lies on the southwestern part of the main island of Mahé, a granite island with dense rainforests. Sea turtles like the hawksbill, as well as tortoises such as the Seychelles giant land tortoise come to its wonderfully wide, sandy beach to lay their eggs. The waves are sometimes rather big, which guarantees that more experienced swimmers will have lots of fun.

Île Coco, The Seychelles
(below)

The tiny island of Île Coco is neighbour to La Digue and one of a total of 115 islands that are part of this island state in the Indian Ocean. However, it is a nature reserve and visitors may not stop there. Anchoring, diving and snorkelling are strictly prohibited. But you'll get fabulous views of the island's heavenly beaches from a boat.

Anse la Réunion, La Digue
(upper left)

La Réunion is the main town on the island of La Digue in the Seychelles. La Digue's lush plant life and countless picture perfect beaches warrant a longer stay. An offshore coral reef near Anse la Réunion on the west side of the island breaks the waves, making it possible to swim and snorkel here under extra safe conditions.

Anse Source d'Argent, La Digue
(upper right)

The magnificent beach on La Digue, called Source d'Argent (EN: silver spring), may seem familiar to lots of telly viewers from the many advertisements filmed there. But in spite of being famous, the beach is a rather peaceful spot. Its massive granite formations are millions of years old. They divide the beach into little coves and create an almost meditative impression.

Anse Sévère, La Digue *(above)*

There's a bay on the west side of La Digue, just a few minutes walk from the village of La Passe. But unlike many others in the Seychelles, it does not have granite rocks. Nevertheless, its fine white sand beach and tropical vegetation are absolutely heavenly. The sunsets here are a special treat. If you're lucky, you'll spot the "green glow" shortly after the sun disappears.

Anse Cocos, La Digue *(below)*

Anse Cocos lies in the southeastern part of La Digue Island. Like so many others you'll find in the Seychelles, the bay has a superb beach. Yet in spite of its heavenly appearance, you have to take care during the Southeast Monsoon. Anse Cocos has no offshore coral reefs, so the waves hit the shore with unbridled force. This is also the case at the neighbouring beaches of Petite Anse and Grande Anse.

La Réunion

Petite-Île, Saint-Pierre
(above)

The island of La Réunion is a French overseas department that lies in the Indian Ocean about 800 km east of Madagascar. La Réunion is 2,512 km² in size and has recently become a favourite holiday destination. The little village of Petite-Île is located in the wild southern part of the island. You can reach Grand Anse by auto from there in just five minutes. This very dreamy bay has turquoise-blue water, lush palms, and a natural stone basin.

Saint Gilles, Saint-Paul
(centre)

Saint Gilles lies on the west coast of the island. This town is a much frequented tourist centre with plenty of hotels, a well developed infrastructure, and ideal beaches at no extra charge. Roches Noires Beach is especially popular with surfers. Back on land you can visit the Jardin d'Eden, a botanical garden and veritable plant paradise.

Boucan Canot, Saint-Paul
(below)

Boucan Canot is a popular seaside resort on the west side of La Réunion. The beach is divided in two: one section is just a bathing beach, while the other is reserved for surfing. Since no offshore coral reef holds back the sea, the water is much deeper here. When the sun sets over the Indian Ocean in the evening, you can celebrate the close of day with a cocktail at the beach bar.

Mauritius

Flic en Flac, Black River *(above)*

This narrow beach in the western part of Mauritius seems to go on forever, yet it only extends for 6 km. There's a coral reef about 100 m offshore that protects the beach, so even inexperienced swimmers can risk going in the water. The little fishing village got its unusual name from Dutch settlers: Flic en Flac means "free and flat land".

Île aux Cerfs, Flacq *(below)*

Île aux Cerfs (EN: deer island) is a small island in the Indian Ocean east of Mauritius. It is uninhabited, but can easily be reached from Mauritius by boat. The island is a favourite bathing spot, which will hardly surprise you when you set eyes on the snow white beaches and turquoise water! The island also has a very exclusive golf course with ocean views.

Cape Verde

Santa Maria, Sal *(above)*

The 30 km long and 12 km wide island of Sal is one of three sand islands in the Cape Verdes. Its white sand beaches draw the largest portion of visitors to this island state in the Atlantic. Sal got its name from the island's rich salt deposits. Offering 350 days of sunshine per year, the little fishing village of Santa Maria in the southern part of the island is a favourite holiday spot.

São Pedro, São Vicente *(centre)*

The islanders of São Vicente live mainly from fishing and tourism. São Pedro is a little fishing village in the southwestern part of the island. Its large sandy beach is a well known gathering place for sea turtles. It is also very popular among wind surfers, because the high waves and rather strong undercurrent in spots make for nothing less than ideal conditions.

Sierra Leone

Lumley
(below)

Sierra Leone has everything from white sand beaches to tropical rainforests – and lots more besides. The coastline of this West African country is 400 km long, and holiday-makers have only recently begun to appreciate it. Tourism is the fastest growing industry in Sierra Leone, a country that was shaken by a bloody civil war from 1991 to 2002.

São Tomé and Príncipe

São Tomé *(lower left)*

The islands of São Tomé and Príncipe lie approximately 140 km apart in the Gulf of Guinea. São Tomé is the capital city of the identically named island. Located in the northeastern part of the island, it was founded by the Portuguese in 1485. Portuguese is still the official language. Yet this West African island has more to offer than heavenly beaches: the gorgeous tropical vegetation of its mountainous interior is very alluring.

Ivory Coast

Abidjan *(above)*

Even in the capital, Abidjan, the beaches of the Ivory Coast shimmer in white ivory tones. The city lies on several peninsulas and islands in the Ébrié Lagoon, and bridges connect them to one another. Abidjan's parks and wide boulevards have earned it the epithet, "Paris of West Africa". Fifty years ago, Abidjan had 50,000 inhabitants. But about five million people now live in this African metropolis.

Ghana

Pleasure Beach, Accra *(LH page)*

West African Ghana is situated just a few degrees north of the equator. It borders the Ivory Coast to the west, Burkina Faso to the north, Togo to the east, and the Gulf of Guinea to the south. You will find superb beaches along its flat, sandy coastline. These beaches are drawing more and more tourist traffic, especially from Europe. And one of them is charming Pleasure Beach near the capital, Accra.

St. Helena

Ascension *(lower right)*

In 1503, the Portuguese seafarer Alphonse d'Albuquerque discovered an island about 1,600 km off the coast of Angola on Ascension Day. Thus, he named it Assunção, which means Ascension in Portuguese. This 91 km² volcanic island in the South Atlantic is now part of the British Overseas Territory of St. Helena. It is a veritable paradise for sea birds, sea turtles, and tropical fish like the black triggerfish.

Namibia

Cape Cross, Erongo *(above)*

Lying in the South Atlantic, Cape Cross is a favourite tourist destination with one of the largest accessible colonies of South African fur seals on Earth. Up to 250,000 animals live here. They bring their young into the world in October and November. Although these animals are fascinating to watch, Namibian fishermen are less enamoured with them, because they decimate the fish population.

Walvis Bay, Erongo *(below)*

The coastal city of Walvis Bay was under South African control until 1994. Today it is mainly known for its abundance of birds. Flamingoes and pelicans are among the over 120,000 birds that live here year round. Another 200,000 migratory birds pass through seasonally. Their living space is a gigantic natural lagoon that lies in Walvis Bay. Dune 7, the highest sand dune in the region, affords you a glorious view of this birders' paradise.

South Africa

Langebaan, Western Cape
(above)

Located about 120 km north of Cape Town, Langebaan Lagoon is the centrepiece of West Coast National Park. The reserve extends along both sides of the 25 km long lagoon, whose azure waters, protected islands and wide marshlands are home to thousands of birds. The seemingly endless, pristine beaches will surely delight visitors, too.

Derde Steen, Western Cape
(below)

Gorgeous Derde Steen Beach is usually deserted. You get there via the West Coast Road from Cape Town. But other "strollers" have discovered its fine white sands and crystal clear water, which is why you'll often come across penguins on this beach. They are completely unperturbed by the wind and kite surfers, who find conditions to their liking on many occasions.

Bloubergstrand, Western Cape
(above)

The Cape Town suburb of Bloubergstrand is not only known for its superb white beaches, but also for its fabulous views. From this vantage point, the gorgeous panorama of Table Mountain will simply astound you. This flat-topped mountain is the region's most famous landmark and may well be the most frequently photographed image in all of South Africa.

Camps Bay, Western Cape
(below)

The palm-fringed beach in the luxurious suburb of Camps Bay not only attracts Cape Town's elite, but lots of holidaymakers as well. From the beach you can see the Twelve Apostles, a mountain range on the Atlantic side of Table Mountain. The beach promenade at Camps Bay is lined with pretty street cafés and little shops.

Sandy Bay, Western Cape
(above)

Sandy Bay lies near Hout Bay on the road between Cape Town and Cape Point. It is one of the last untouched sections of coastline on the Cape. If you want to get there, you must first make your way through the steep dunes and bushy slopes. But your efforts will be rewarded by the magnificent view of a peaceful beach with rocky ledges jutting out into the sea.

Muizenberg, Western Cape
(below)

The popular seaside resort of Muizenberg, a suburb of Cape Town, lies where the coastline of the Cape Peninsula turns toward False Bay. The beach at False Bay stretches for over 20 km. This is the birthplace of South African surfing. And the swells are so fantastic that it comes as no surprise. Climbers love to test their skills on the steep cliff walls that the rise above Muizenberg.

Silversands Bay, Western Cape
(above)

Silversands is a gorgeous bay in the Western Cape Province. And it surely lives up to its name, for its sands shimmer silvery-white in the South African sun. You can take long walks on the beach, or just enjoy the sun and sea. There's a good spot for diving on the east side of the beach where you can explore the bay's richly diverse underwater world.

Boulders Beach, Western Cape
(below)

Boulders Beach in Boulders National Park is not only known for its small, isolated bays with white sands and calm waters; its large colony of African penguins is even more famous. About 3,000 of these comical birds live at nearby Foxy Beach. Granite boulders shape the look of Boulder Beach and give the park its name.

Herolds Bay, Western Cape
(above)

Protected by surrounding cliffs, Herolds Bay lies about 15 km west of George. Its golden sands and typical Cape landscape of rich fynbos vegetation make it an ideal location for beach fans and nature lovers. Many species of sea birds, weaver birds, and finches brood here. Whilst strolling along the coast, you will often spot whales and dolphins.

Port Alfred, Eastern Cape
(centre)

Port Alfred lies at the mouth of the Kowie River, almost halfway between the cities of Port Elizabeth and East London. This small town has Kelly's Beach, one of the most beautiful in South Africa. There are two swim platforms from which visitors can enjoy watching bathers, whales, or the glorious sunsets. And if you prefer something more active, you can indulge in numerous water sports from diving to canoeing.

Durban, KwaZulu-Natal
(below)

With about 3.2 million inhabitants, Durban is the second largest city in South Africa. Its subtropical climate and superb, Indian Ocean beaches have made it a favourite destination for sun worshipers, swimmers and surfers. There's always a lot going on along the Golden Mile, a prime beachfront area with a street and promenade. But if you're looking for peace and quiet, there is also a secluded beach right nearby.

NORTH AND SOUTH AMERICA

UNPARALLED BEACHES

North America is commonly described as a continent of superlatives. In any case, the diversity of its landscapes may well break all records. North America has more variety on offer than any other continent. Just imagine Alaska's raw beauty, the wide open expanses of Canada, charming New England fishing villages, the magic of Indian Summer in the Great Lakes Region, and the wild Northwestern portion of the USA. We must also link up fascinating dream destinations in the south, such as America's most beautiful sandbox, "The Sunshine State" of Florida, and California's Pacific coastline – where life is always being played out at the beach. And we must surely include the spectacular Hawaiian Islands, whose very name evokes wanderlust.

Awaiting you in Central America are tropical rain forests, fascinating flora and fauna, the legacies of the once influential Mayan culture, and heavenly beaches. The unique face of this continent is a combination of many different coastlines and the oceans that border them: the Atlantic, the Pacific, the Caribbean, and the polar seas.

Canada

Hopewell Rocks, Bay of Fundy, New Brunswick *(above)*

"Flowerpot Rocks" is the nickname of this rock formation in New Brunswick Province. And if you look closely at these rocks in the Bay of Fundy, the reason becomes clear. Their odd shapes came about through the erosive force of the water. The Bay of Fundy has highest tidal range (16 m) in the world. The lower half of the rock formation is under water at high tide.

St. Peters Island, Prince Edward Island *(below)*

Prince Edward Island, the smallest Canadian province, is situated in the Gulf of Saint Lawrence on the east coast of North America. It is comprised of numerous islands, including picturesque St. Peters Island. Like the entire region, this island is famous for its beautiful landscapes and peaceful seclusion. The best way to see it is by kayak.

Peggy's Cove, Nova Scotia
(upper left)

The little fishing village of Peggy's Cove lies 43 km southwest of Halifax and is one of the main highlights of a visit to the province of Nova Scotia. Peggy's Cove is also on the Lighthouse Trail, an excursion route that runs past numerous lighthouses and coastal villages. The venerable lighthouse at Peggy's Point sits atop a granite promontory, and you'll get a superb view of the Atlantic from there.

Blomidon, Nova Scotia
(lower left)

Blomidon lies about 100 km west of Halifax at Minas Basin in the Bay of Fundy. Blomidon's steep cliffs and intermittently rocky beaches make for impressive landscapes that will surely fascinate nature lovers. The cliffs can reach heights of up to 180 m. Hiking in the hinterlands or along the coast will take you to a multitude of geological formations and interesting layers of sedimentary rock.

Black Bay, Lake Superior, Ontario *(lower RH page)*

Lake Superior lies on the border of the USA and Canada. Covering an area of 82,413 km², it is the largest of North America's five Great Lakes and has outstanding water quality. In terms of surface area, Lake Superior is the world's second largest lake, the largest being the Caspian Sea. The Black Bay Peninsula has a picturesque coastline with lots of little offshore islands.

Vancouver, British Columbia
(above)

Located in the province of British Columbia on Canada's west coast, the bustling metropolis of Vancouver rates as one of the best cities in the world for quality of life. Its beaches stretch along the Pacific coast for a total of 18 km, adding significant recreational value to the equation. Sailing and beach volleyball are the passions here. The Rocky Mountains beckon to hikers and skiers from a distance.

USA

Cape Cod, Massachusetts
(upper RH page)

This 1,033 km² peninsula in southeastern Massachusetts has been separated from the American mainland since 1914. Cape Cod is a favourite, summertime holiday spot. Its endless beaches foster rest and recreation. The soft pastel light draws many illustrators and painters to the Cape. Whale watching tours provide an opportunity to observe humpback and fin whales.

Nantucket, Massachusetts
(above)

The seaside and health resort of Nantucket is an oasis of peace. The gentle dunes and marvellous waves of Surfside Beach lie on the south coast. Also worth visiting are Sconset Beach on the east coast and the lighthouse at Great Point. Surfers will find ideal conditions, particularly at Madaquecham Beach.

Martha's Vineyard, Massachusetts *(lower left)*

The 231 km² island of Martha's Vineyard is a luxurious holiday resort for overworked urbanites. Anyone seeking rest and relaxation will find it here. Lots of American Presidents have been fond of the beaches on this island. So it is that the Kennedy family, among others, has had a summer residence on Martha's Vineyard for decades. Gay Head Beach has fabulous, multi-coloured cliffs and is the right spot for long, solitary walks along the shore.

Coney Island Beach, New York
(lower rt./LH page)

Coney Island is a peninsula at the southern tip of Long Island on the Atlantic. It was already a popular seaside resort for New Yorkers in the nineteenth century. In subsequent years, a number of amusement parks were established here. Most of them have since disappeared, and the charm of old Coney Island along with them. Yet the beach and boardwalk get lots of visitors on hot summer days.

Silver Lake, Little Sable Point Light, Michigan *(below)*

Situated on the east coast of Lake Michigan is an 8 km² area of dunes called Silver Lake State Park. People simply love this beach, and it doesn't matter whether they use it for sunbathing and swimming by day, or for watching the spectacular sunsets in the evening. Built in the 1870s, Little Sable Point Light is a red brick lighthouse that has been taken out of service and now houses a small museum.

Oak Street Beach, Chicago, Illinois *(above)*

The third largest city in the USA is chiefly a financial centre and transport hub. But you can still loll about on a sunny beach in Chicago. Oak Street Beach lies on the shore of Lake Michigan, directly north of the city's most elegant street, the Magnificent Mile. Skyscrapers in the background and the golden sandy beach make for a unique atmosphere.

Virginia Beach, Virginia *(centre)*

The popular holiday resort of Virginia Beach lies in Chesapeake Bay. This beach on the Atlantic has even managed an entry in the Guinness Book of Records. That's because Virginia Beach is the longest recreational beach in the world. Hundreds of hotels, motels, and restaurants along a 45 km stretch of beach make this an exciting holiday destination. The lighthouse at Cape Henry is a special high point of this record-setting beach.

Cape Hatteras, North Carolina *(lower RH page)*

The Outer Banks form a narrow, elongated chain of islands along the Atlantic coastline of North Carolina. At Cape Hatteras, you'll find pristine beaches, dunes, and marshes that offer sanctuary to sea turtles and a multitude of aquatic birds. Each visit to the Cape is a novel experience, because tides, strong currents, and hefty winds ensure that things are always in flux.

Daytona Beach, Florida
(above)

What's unique here is that even cars and motorcycles can drive, albeit slowly, the 37 km length of Daytona Beach. Those who come to Daytona are seeking "action" in the form of surfing, sunbathing, and nightlife. Daytona Beach is notorious for "spring break", when some 200,000 students come from all over the U.S. to celebrate the arrival of spring with wild parties.

Boca Raton, Florida
(lower LH page)

Boca Raton is about 60 km north of Miami. Its long beach is bordered by various parks, and rock formations at the south end of Red Reef Park provide good snorkelling. You've got water on both sides at Spanish River Park: a lagoon to the west, and the Atlantic to the east.

Fort Lauderdale, Florida
(lower left)

Anyone who wants to escape hectic Miami can slip over to Fort Lauderdale. The shallow water along South Ocean Drive is outstanding for swimming, surfing, and sailing. Canals traverse the city, which is known as the Venice of America. Fort Lauderdale also has one of the largest yacht harbours in the world.

Miami Beach, Florida
(lower right)

Miami Beach lies on a peninsula to the north of the city proper. Due to its subtropical climate, this 16 km beach is busy all year round. Time and again, the city has had to deposit more sand on this beach to make up for erosion. In contrast to the financial metropolis of Miami, you can enjoy an extensive beach culture and nightlife here.

Miami, Florida
(above)

With about two million residents, Miami is Florida's biggest city. A large portion of the city stretches along the coastline of Biscayne Bay. Several hundred islands lie in the bay. Its tropical climate, sunny beaches, and the lively Cuban flair of Calle Ocho lure lots of visitors to Miami.

Key Biscayne, Florida
(above)

Key Biscayne is an island south of Miami Beach. The Atlantic borders it on the east, Biscayne Bay on the west, and a causeway connects it to Miami. Anyone who comes here has several beaches from which to choose. The 5 km long beach at Crandon Park has the most impressive scenery and lies in the northern part of the island. Lighthouse enthusiasts will find the picturesque, white Cape Florida Light (1825) at the south end of Key Biscayne.

Ocean Drive, Miami Beach, Florida *(below)*

Ocean Drive leads along the coastline of Miami Beach. South Beach is, without a doubt, the city's upscale shopping district. This road is famous for lots of interesting art deco buildings that are bathed in soft pastel tones and radiate southern joie de vivre.

Key West, Florida
(above)

The city of Key West lies at the southernmost point of the Florida Keys and is also the southernmost city in the USA. Famous writers like Ernest Hemingway and Tennessee Williams were drawn here by the Cuban atmosphere and the plethora of bars. South Beach is Key West's best-known beach. This is where people celebrate the sunset each and every night with a beach party.

Naples, Florida
(below)

Along with Marco Island and Everglades National Park, Naples is part of South Florida's Paradise Coast. The city has 22,000 residents. Upon seeing the radiant white sand at beautiful, 16 km long Naples Beach, people surely feel as though they've arrived in Paradise. In 2005, this beach was named the most beautiful in the USA by the Travel Channel, a cable and satellite television channel.

Sanibel und Captiva Islands, Florida *(upper RH page)*

Captiva Island was originally part of Sanibel Island, but a hurricane divided them in two. Both of these islands off the coast of Fort Myers have long beaches with remarkable shell deposits. In fact, Sanibel's Bailey-Matthews Shell Museum is dedicated to conchology. You should take alligator crossing signs seriously, because encounters between people and alligators are not at all rare here.

Fort Myers, Florida *(centre)*

Life is more peaceful and relaxed in Fort Myers on Florida's west coast than in the rest of the state. Estero Island is the city's longest offshore island. This is where you can fully enjoy the gloriously soft sand and turquoise green waters of the Gulf of Mexico. And you'll experience particularly picturesque sunsets on any of the hundreds of uninhabited, offshore islands.

Panama City, Florida *(below)*

Panama City in Northwest Florida is famous for its beautiful beaches and unabashedly advertizes them as "the world's most beautiful beaches". The colour of the clear water has also earned the coastline the epithet, The Emerald Coast. The glittering white sands are made of little quartz crystals that have washed down from the Appalachian Mountains.

Clearwater Beach, Florida
(above)

Clearwater Beach lies on the Pinellas Peninsula. This part of Florida's west coast gets 361 days of sunshine per year, and so Clearwater Beach has been entered into the Guinness Book of Records. Two of its beaches are consistently ranked among the most beautiful in the U.S. And the region can pride itself on the fact that it has a beach with endless white sands and turquoise green water that stretches along the Gulf of Mexico for over 50 km.

Barrow, Alaska
(lower left)

The northernmost beach on the American continent is only a beach in high summer. During the rest of the year, the City of Barrow is surrounded by drift and pack ice from the Arctic Ocean. The approximately 2,000 inhabitants live from whaling, salmon fishing, and tourism. Holidaymakers cross the Arctic Circle so that they can see what it's like to be at the edge of the world. Most of them travel by plane.

First Beach, Olympic National Park, Washington *(lower right)*

Although Olympic National Park in America's Pacific Northwest is known for its temperate rainforests, there's lots more to discover here. After a short walk through the forest, you'll come to First Beach, a solitary beach littered with driftwood and rocks. And watching the sun set over the Pacific waves at First Beach is a magical experience.

Cove Beach, Oregon *(above)*

When the weather in other parts of the region is not especially suited to swimming, you can still bathe at Cove Beach. That's because the beach is on the leeward side of Cape Perpetua, and even when the wind is blowing hard, it stays nice and warm in this spot. Since the beach is almost completely flooded at high tide and only accessible at low tide, the dunes that lie behind it offer a welcome alternative for sun worshippers.

Baker Beach, San Francisco, California *(below)*

Baker Beach is approximately 800 m long and begins at the point where the Golden Gate Bridge meets the San Francisco Peninsula. The beach is part of The Presidio of San Francisco. A military fortress was built on this site in 1776. The sandy beach offers plenty of room for swimming and sunbathing, and you should definitely take in the wonderful view of Golden Gate Bridge.

Bandon Beach State Park, Oregon *(upper left)*

The Coquille River spills into the Pacific at the little fishing village of Bandon. Jagged rock formations rise up just offshore from the beach. One of them is Face Rock which, according to legend, is that of an Indian maiden who was turned to stone by an evil spirit. From the rocks off Sunset Beach, you can watch the seals when they take a rest here from time to time.

Cannon Beach, Oregon *(lower left)*

Cannon Beach in the Pacific Northwest is Oregon's favourite beach. Despite the rather large number of visitors, this little town with a 12 km stretch of sandy beach has a pleasant atmosphere. Haystack Rock, a great coastal monolith that towers to a height of 72 m, lies just off shore, and there is a little cave system inside it.

Pebble Beach, California *(upper right)*

Pebble Beach is not a city, but rather a quiet, very exclusive private community in Monterey County that belongs to the Pebble Beach Company. Pebble Beach has a total of seven, eighteen hole golf courses and is, therefore, known mainly to golfers. But you can also drop by the beach, where the sometimes gentle, sometimes powerful waves of the Pacific invite you for a swim.

Santa Cruz, California
(above)

Santa Cruz was supposedly the first beach on which people surfed in California. They say that three Hawaiian princes got on their boards here in 1885. Even today, surfing is a big deal in Santa Cruz. This city on Monterey Bay is about 115 km south of San Francisco and has a total of eleven beaches with excellent surfing conditions.

Carmel River State Beach, California *(below)*

Splendid Carmel River State Beach extends for about 1.5 km near the city of Carmel at the north end of Big Sur on the Central Coast. The Carmel River forms a lagoon, and lots of migratory birds stop here to break up their journeys. No matter how picturesque the beach may seem, the peacefulness here is deceptive. On account of the strong currents, swimming can be very dangerous here.

Big Sur, California *(above)*

Big Sur (EN: Great South) is the name of a 90 km long stretch of coastline between San Simeon and Carmel. This is where the Pacific Coast Highway runs right along the Pacific coast. It is one of the most beautiful drives in the world, a breath-taking mixture of cliffs, mountains, coves, and ocean. With a bit of luck, you'll be able to spot a grey whale or sea lion from your car.

Santa Barbara, California *(below)*

The coastline around Santa Barbara is called the American Riviera. Located about 160 km northwest of Los Angeles, Santa Barbara has 93,000 residents. Anyone driving along the coast will come across one splendid villa after another, as well as yacht harbours and beaches that could just as well lie on the Mediterranean. The Santa Ynez Mountains loom directly behind the city, reaching heights of up to 1,200 m.

Santa Monica, California
(above)

Located in the bay of the same name, Santa Monica lies in the midst of steep cliffs that stretch out along the Pacific. The fine white sand beach and mountainous hinterland are an absolute must for any visit to California. The city's famous landmark, the Santa Monica Pier, was built in the 1920s. The pier and its amusement park have been the setting for countless Hollywood movies.

Malibu, Los Angeles, California
(below)

Anyone who hears the word, Malibu, will automatically think of the television series, *Baywatch*. And lots of film stars actually do live in this Los Angeles suburb, many of them in stilt houses that lie directly on one of Malibu's famous beaches. You can watch world famous surfers at Surfrider Beach. And so it's entirely appropriate for coveted, local license plates to read, Malibu: A Way of Life.

Venice Beach, California
(above)

Originally built as a holiday resort by a tobacco millionaire, this 4.5 km stretch of sandy beach is now very popular with swimmers and surfers alike. Sport enthusiasts have a veritable open air fitness studio on Ocean Front Walk, which is the local boardwalk. Lots of street artists, musicians, painters, and athletes romp around Venice Beach at the weekend.

San Diego, California
(centre)

With 1.2 million residents, San Diego is California's second largest city. It sits at the southwesternmost corner of the United States. The Mediterranean climate and kilometre long beaches have caused the population to surge by leaps and bounds in recent years. The many festivals that reflect San Diego's Mexican heritage also draw lots of visitors.

South Laguna Beach, California
(below)

Even apart from its picturesque coastline, the artist colony of Laguna Beach and its 24,000 residents have quite a few things on offer, including a number of art galleries, the Laguna Art Museum, and three large summer festivals. The beach invites you to relax. Painters are anything but scarce at South Laguna Beach. They try to capture the warm light and colours of the California sun.

Huntington Beach, California
(above)

Surf City is the nickname given to Huntington Beach in Southern California's Orange County. And it is no exaggeration to say that surfing looms large here. Locals are not the only ones spending every free minute on their boards, for this city also hosts international surfing championships. Fantastic waves on a 14 km stretch of beach make all of this possible!

Main Beach, Laguna Beach, California *(below)*

The coves, gentle beaches, rocky promontories, and rock-studded ocean at Laguna Beach are somewhat reminiscent of the French Riviera. This popular, Orange County seaside resort and its several beaches are ready to receive you. One of them is Main Beach, and you can watch unforgettable sunsets over the Pacific from there.

Queen's Bath, Kauai, Hawaii
(above)

This royal bathing beach really lives up to its name. It lies in a small, shallow bay that is separated from the south end of Polihale Beach by a reef. The bay is protected from high waves and strong ocean currents, making it an exceptionally safe place for swimmers. Queen's Bath lies on the west side of Kauai and can only be reached via an unpaved road.

Polihale, Kauai, Hawaii
(lower LH page)

Polihale is a heavenly, outlying beach on the west side of Kauai in the Hawaiian Islands. Over the course of several kilometres, the golden sands call you to sunbathe and swim. This beach plays a special role in Hawaiian mythology: spirits of the deceased apparently reach the afterworld by jumping into the sea from the surrounding cliffs.

Yokohama Bay, Oahu, Hawaii
(above)

Japanese settlers worked here in the sugar cane fields. And they named this bay on Oahu's northwest coast after their home town of Yokohama. Visitors to this remote stretch of coastline will find a true paradise of deserted beaches, dunes, rocky cliffs and, needless to say, deep blue water. With a bit of luck, you may even catch sight of dolphins in the bay.

Waikiki Beach, Oahu, Hawaii
(below)

Waikiki is a district of Honolulu on the southern coast of Oahu. Its shimmering golden beach is one of the most famous in the world. About 65,000 people come here every day to surf, swim in the ocean, or loll about in the sun. A statue of Duke Kahanomoku commemorates the athlete who invented the crawl stroke and popularised surfing.

Napili Beach, Maui, Hawaii
(above)

The soft, snow white sands of Napili Beach glisten like gold at sunrise. This 800 m long beach on the west coast of Maui is protected by a coral reef, so even in winter the waves never get too high. It is fabulous for swimming and snorkelling. The likelihood of encountering sea turtles is also fairly high.

Big Beach, Maui, Hawaii
(below)

Makena Beach is the official name of this wonderful stretch of sand on the southern coast of Maui. It is one of most famous beaches in the Hawaiian Islands. And Makena really is a picture perfect beach with fine, white sand and beautiful turquoise water. Divers and snorkelers may catch sight of various species of butterfly fish.

Mexico

San Felipe, Baja California
(above)

The seaside resort of San Felipe lies on a peninsula called Baja California. Since it's right on the California border, the peninsula is a favourite holiday destination for many Americans. Despite the lively beach culture and recreational packages for water skiing and catamaran sailing, the beach at San Felipe is an exceptionally idyllic spot in the evening. As the sun goes down against a peach-coloured sky, it bathes the sea in bright violet hues.

Puerto Vallarta, Jalisco *(below)*

Puerto Vallarta is currently one of Mexico's largest Pacific Ocean resorts. Yet in spite of everything, this former fishing village has preserved its original charm: simply note the red tiled roofs, brightly whitewashed houses, and many excellent beaches. Playa Mismaloya became world famous as the idyllic setting for the movie, *The Night of the Iguana* (1964), with Liz Taylor and Richard Burton.

Acapulco, Guerrero (above)

With 16 km of sandy beaches and opulent watersport offerings, Acapulco is a fashionable beach resort par excellence. You'll come upon lively beaches in the bay, one of which is Playa Paraiso. But you'll also find peaceful fishing villages like Puerto Marques. And don't miss the cliff divers, a group of professional divers who plunge head first into the Pacific from the cliffs at La Quebrada.

Cancun, Quintana Roo (below)

The popular holiday paradise of Cancun lies at the centre of the Mayan Riviera that runs along the Caribbean coastline of southeast Mexico. Along with famous Mayan archaeological sites, this city on the Yucatán Peninsula offers sunny white beaches and turquoise water. Conditions at Cancun are perfect for diving, windsurfing, and deep sea fishing.

Sian Ka'an, Quintana Roo
(above)

The Sian Ka'an Biosphere Reserve is near Tulum. Visitors who wish to turn their back on civilisation for a bit will enjoy its natural palm forests and deserted coral beaches with crystal clear water. Flamingos, parrots, spider monkeys, and turtles make their home here. And it's certainly worth visiting secluded Boca de Paila, which lies on a small peninsula within the biosphere reserve.

Playa Akumal, Quintana Roo
(below)

The Yacatán Peninsula combines ancient culture with the natural beauty of the Caribbean, and it does so within the smallest possible area. Playa Akumal on the Mayan Riviera is a snow white, palm-lined beach that is perfectly suited for sunbathing and snorkelling in the deep blue sea. Yet you can also visit the mysterious Mayan ruins, which are just a stone's throw from this heavenly beach.

Belize

Goff's Caye, Belize (above)

The boat ride from Belize City to Goff's Caye takes about forty-five minutes. The ocean surrounding this tiny barrier island shimmers in every Caribbean colour from bright green to deep blue. Visitors can enjoy the sunny weather from beneath one of the beach's thirteen coconut palms, or explore the world's second largest coral reef. Just put on a mask and flippers, and snorkel away!

Honduras

Cayos Cochinos, Islas de la Bahía (below)

The Islas de la Bahía lie off the coast of Honduras. Fine shell sand and shimmering, Caribbean turquoise seas are typical of these islands. Cayos Cochinos belongs to the Bahía Archipelago. The coral reefs that surround it are pristine, and the biodiversity is outstanding on both land and sea. Encounters with colourful parrots and numerous species of reptiles are an everyday occurrence here.

Nicaragua

Masachapa, Managua *(above)*

Wide beaches, pristine natural surroundings, and glorious sunsets are all good reasons to visit the fishing village of Masachapa. Proximity to Managua and the chance to master Pacific beaches on horseback also speak in favour of this holiday resort. The beaches are mostly deserted, and the gentle swells offer ideal conditions for learning how to surf.

San Juan del Sur, Rivas *(below)*

The beach paradise of San Juan del Sur lies on a crescent shaped bay in southern Nicaragua. Cliffs and mountains surround the bay. This quiet little town on the Pacific is just a few kilometres from the Costa Rican border and is a very inviting place to surf or fish. You'll find rows of little eateries along the beach promenade. The many fishing boats in the harbour are a lovely sight at sunset.

Costa Rica

Guanacaste National Park
(above)

Whether on land or sea, pristine nature is the hallmark of Guanacaste National Park in Costa Rica's far north. Anyone adventurous enough to end up in this remarkable place will be able to hike through the cloud forest, enjoy the heavenly Pacific beaches, or rub shoulders with reef sharks, eagle rays, and cuttlefish while diving past volcanic rocks.

Puntarenas *(upper RH page)*

Puntarenas sits on a promontory that soars above the Pacific Ocean. The harbour is a popular stopover for cruise ships, so the beach gets very crowded, especially at the weekend. But you can still experience quiet sunsets at Puntarenas. Tours to the islands in the Gulf of Nicoya depart from Puntarenas, which is also the capital of Puntarenas Province.

Playa Carrillo, Guanacaste
(lower rt./RH page)

Playa Carrillo lies in an elongated bay on the Pacific coast of northwestern Costa Rica, just a few kilometres south of the little town of Samsara. A coral reef surrounds the beach. What a wonderful spot for bathing and snorkelling! At sunset, Playa Carrillo makes the perfect spot to end the day with a Sundowner.

Manuel Antonio National Park, Puntarenas *(lower l./RH page)*

Manuel Antonio National Park is one of southern Cost Rica's most idyllic holiday spots. This pristine, natural setting includes twelve, offshore islands and palm forests along the Pacific coast. Every so often, whales surface near the beautiful beaches and with a bit of luck, you may even spot them there. Also highly recommended is a day trip to the rain forest, which is home to coatis, iguanas, capuchin monkeys, and armadillos.

Playa Espadilla, Puntarenas
(above)

Visitors who wish for a mix of sunny tropical beaches and shadowy rainforest canopies will find Playa Espadilla just right. This long beach near Manuel Antonio National Park is perfectly suited for long walks and sunbathing. But the strong currents make it a bit risky for water sports.

Tortuguero National Park, Limón *(centre)*

The canals and lagoons of Tortuguero National Park make it one of the most popular excursion destinations on Costa Rica's Caribbean coastline. You can only get there by plane or boat, however. Year after year, sea turtles come onto this tropical beach to lay their eggs, and the park is named after them. Crocodiles and caimans live in the lagoons, and you should avoid coming into close contact with them.

Cahuita National Park, Limón
(below)

Punta Cahuita lies on a little promontory between the Caribbean coastline and the rainforest. It has endless palm beaches and colourful coral gardens in which sea turtles and lobsters cavort. Monkeys, sloths, iguanas, and colourful tropical butterflies live in the mangrove swamps and rainforests of Cahuita National Park.

Panama

San Blas, Kuna Yala *(above)*

The San Blas Archipelago lies on the south-east coast of Panama. It consists of approx. 365 tropical palm islands, and sailors love to head for them. In view of the many islands, there are reefs and beaches to suit nearly every taste. Visitors to this archipelago stay in huts near the native Kuna Indians, which gives them a chance to learn about tradition-al island ways.

Los Grillos, Rio Sidra *(below)*

The Panamanian offshore island of Rio Sidra is a Caribbean jewel. Every advantage of a heavenly isle comes together in this tiniest of spaces: utter stillness, coconut palms swaying in the wind, sparkling water with colourful fish, and a beach you can stroll on with ease. It's the ideal spot for people who want to get away from the daily grind.

THE CARIBBEAN

HEAVENLY ISLANDS, RELAXED LIFESTYLE

Radiant red Royal Poinciana and hibiscus blossoms, lush green rainforests, houses in pastels, blinding white beaches, and oceans shimmering in every shade of blue: these are the colours of the Caribbean. And sometimes the world of coral reefs is even more colourful than what you see on land. "The most beautiful coast ever beheld by the human eye," said Christopher Columbus about the Dominican Republic. He discovered the island in 1492 and named it Hispania. This is where the longest beaches in the Caribbean are found. On the other hand, the island nation of Antigua and Barbuda has 365 beaches, one for each day of the year. And let's not dismiss the other islands of the Greater and Lesser Antilles: Salsa-style holidays in Cuba, the picturesque bays of the Virgin Islands, the wild beauty of Dominica, British-influenced Barbados, the famous ABC islands of Aruba, Bonaire and Curaçao off the coast of Venezuela, the spice island of Grenada, the Pitons of St. Lucia that are visible for miles around, Trinidad with its calypso Carnival celebration, and Guadeloupe, which unites French élan with Caribbean temperament like no other island. Added to that are Jamaica, The Bahamas, Anguilla, St. Kitts and Nevis, The Bermudas, Martinique, The Grenadines, and Puerto Rico – and the list goes on and on. Yet there are still those quiet places where you can find your centre amid rustling palms and rushing seas.

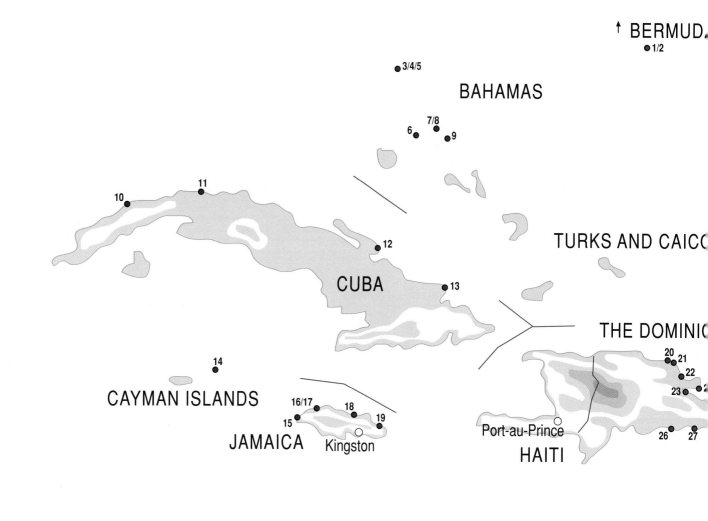

Bermuda

Warwick *(upper RH page)*

The Bermudas are also known as pink paradise on account of their unusual beaches, which are coloured pink with the dust from shells and coral. Holiday guests will find the most intense shade of pink at Warwick Beach. This stretch of beach also features rum swizzle samples, the national drink of the Bermudas.

Southampton *(upper left)*

The elegant Southampton Hotel lies on the south coast of Main Island, which is connected to the other islands by seven bridges. Stars like Bette Midler have stayed there, and it still has a very British feel. From this hilly vantage point, guests can let their gaze wander over the pink sands either before or after five o'clock tea.

The Bahamas

Guana Cay, Abaco *(lower left)*

Once they've discovered the beach at Guana Cay, sun worshippers will surely spend their entire holiday on this promontory in the Abaco Islands. The fine grain sand is pink, and the water shimmers in blue and turquoise shades that are nowhere more beautiful than here. The beach also offers a 12 km stretch for extensive strolling.

Hope Town, Abaco *(below)*

Hope Town on Elbow Cay was founded by British loyalists. Small beaches, houses with pastel facades, plus a red and white stripe lighthouse at the entrance to the harbour make it one of the loveliest hamlets in the Bahamas. The observation deck at the lighthouse offers an exclusive panorama of this idyllic little city and harbour bay.

Treasure Cay, Abaco *(above)*

A gorgeous beach called Treasure Cay lies north of March Harbour on Great Abaco Island. Powdery sand, coconut palms, plus shallow water for bathing and snorkelling make this a very high-end, 5 km stretch of sand. Anyone who isn't sailing in the Abacos, which are known as the sailing capital of the world, can always have a look at the boats in the nearby yacht harbour.

Nassau, New Providence *(below)*

Nassau on the island of New Providence is both the capital city and the centre of activity in the Bahamas. It has a harbour for cruise ships, chic restaurants and bars, elegant boutiques, and pretty wooden houses. Around Nassau you'll find well known beaches like Paradise Island, Cable Beach, and Love Beach. They offer a stunning number of recreational activities for holiday guests and for the many day trippers from the cruise ships.

Governor's Harbour, Eleuthera *(lower RH page)*

Sleepy villages, pink sand and pineapple fields are the principal attractions on the long, thin island of Eleuthera. The main town, Governor's Harbour, lies at the centre of the island. Eleuthera is so narrow here that you can go from coast to coast in half an hour and discover many hidden beaches along the way.

Pink Beach, Harbour Island
(above)

The colour of Pink Beach at Harbour Island is reminiscent of pale pink cotton candy. The unusual colouration comes from the fact that the sand is made up of ground coral and various shells, including conch shells. The sight of brilliant pink stretching along dark blue waters for over 4.5 km will literally take your breath away.

Little San Salvador Island *(lower left)*

Little San Salvador Island, also known as Half Moon Cay, is the private property of the Holland America Line and its cruise ship fleet. The island is only for passengers whose ships make a stopover here. This island is an exclusive, dream destination with aquamarine water, a powdered sugar beach, and every imaginable sporting opportunity from sailing and snorkelling to parasailing.

Cuba

Varadero, Matanzas
(above)

The seaside resort of Varadero is Cuba's favourite travel destination. It lies on the north coast about 120 km east of the capital, Havana. Hacienda owners have been building summer villas here since the nineteenth century. Before that, it was a pirate stronghold and shipyard. Today's holiday-makers have laid claim to its fine, white sands and blue green sea.

Santa Maria del Mar, Havana
(below)

Santa Maria del Mar comes just before you reach the gates of Havana. At the weekend, Habañeros roll their highly polished, vintage cars right up to the beach. Bright red and blue automobiles beneath palms are as much a part Cuban life as are its music, rum, and cigars. The largest island in the Caribbean also has powdery white beaches and diving spots with water as warm as a bathtub.

The Cayman Islands

Playa los Cocos, Camagüey
(upper right)

Playa los Cocos, a heavenly, out-of-the-way beach in northern Cuba, lies in a nature reserve and bird sanctuary. It's easily reachable from Playa Santa Lucia and well worth visiting. The water at this beach seems a little more intensely turquoise than elsewhere on the island. And besides, you can snorkel in the crystal clear water and marvel at the intact coral reefs.

Playa Guardalavaca, Holguin
(below)

This powdery white beach looks like the heavenly beaches you see in adverts for Caribbean paradises. Additional advantages of Guardalavaca include the warm transparent water, abundance of coral, and colourful schools of fish. This beach absolutely invites you to enjoy Cuban rhythms and a Cuba Libre beneath a palm tree or a horseback ride along the beach.

Point of Sand, Little Cayman
(upper left)

Point of Sand is an absolutely idyllic holiday spot at the eastern point of Little Cayman that truly lives up to its name. Sun worshippers can enjoy dazzling sand for as far as the eye can see, as well as a fantastic view of the neighbouring island of Cayman Brac at the horizon. It's an ideal place for swimming, snorkelling, and lounging about.

Jamaica

Negril, Westmoreland *(above)*

Located on the western tip of Jamaica, the former hippie and artist colony of Negril has kept its charm. Sun worshippers gather on the endless, more than 10 km long beach, whilst divers meet at Shark's Reef. In the evening, they all gather on the beach or by the cliffs near Rick's Cafe to watch the magnificent sunsets and the high-spirited rock divers.

Montego Bay, St. James *(below)*

Jamaica's fourth largest city, Montego Bay, is located on northwest coast of this island nation. Montego Bay's most famous beach, Doctor's Cave Beach, lies in a protected spot with crystal clear, turquoise water. Surrounded by picturesque hills, it is very popular with photographers. White Sands is almost as popular, and the name alone tells you all you need to know about the gorgeous white beach.

Halfmoon Bay, St. James
(above)

Halfmoon Bay – even the name sounds romantic. This crescent-shaped cove in Montego Bay seems made for intimate togetherness and for couples who want the gentle waves and footprints in the sand all to themselves. Riding through the water on horseback, swimming with dolphins, and a whole range of leisure activities make for lasting memories.

Frenchman's Cove, Portland
(centre)

Frenchman's Cove in northeastern Jamaica is a truly idyllic rainforest. Its magnificent beach lined with almond trees has served as a natural backdrop for many movies. Rafting trips are on offer at nearby Rio Grande. Visitors should be sure to take a refreshing plunge in the blue lagoon, where the snorkelling is also excellent.

Ocho Ríos, St. Ann
(below)

Ocho Ríos is the island's second largest holiday resort. Located on the northern coast of Jamaica, its golden, palm-lined beaches lure European visitors in the main. The nearby landscapes are also extremely attractive. The hills, valleys, plantations, and forests in the foothills of the Dry Harbour Mountains invite long hikes and photographic excursions.

The Dominican Republic

Playa Grande, Rio San Juan
(LH page)

The town of Rio San Juan, its colourful houses, and little shops are distinctly creole. Gri Gri Lagoon is near Playa Grande's palm-lined beaches, and you can explore it by taking a boat trip. These impressive tours lead along serpentine waterways, passing by caves, isolated beaches, and a natural canopy of mangrove forests.

Playa Matancitas, Maria Trinidad Sanchez *(lower left)*

There are lots of gorgeous beaches near Nagua on the northeast coast of the Dominican Republic. You'll find gentle surf, lagoons, and coconut groves at Playa Matancitas, for example. But you must exercise a bit of caution when exploring by car, because local residents frequently place coffee beans and coconuts on the road to dry.

Playa Grande, Maria Trinidad Sanchez *(lower right)*

The Costa Verde coastal road from Cabrera to Rio San Juan skirts dense tropical forests and steep rocks. Playa Grande lies along it in a lovely, protected bay. The beach is a heavenly spot on which to get a tan. You can also sit under shady trees and marvel at the harmonious mix of cliffs and sea.

Costa Esmeralda, Samana *(above)*

Costa Esmeralda gets its name from the sparkling, emerald green waters of Samana Bay. Palm-fringed beaches, mangrove forests, lagoons, and dense jungle are typical of this largely undeveloped stretch of coastline. There are regular sightings of humpback whales in February and March. Rugged individualists will especially enjoy this natural paradise.

El Frances, Santo Domingo
(above)

Idyllic tropical El Frances Beach lies on the southern coast. Its proximity to Santo Domingo makes it a great location for day trips to the bustling metropolis. The cobbled streets, ornate gas lanterns, and palaces of the old town bear witness to its colonial history. And you really should experience the exciting nightlife of Santo Domingo.

Cayo Levantado, Samana
(centre)

The tiny island of Cayo Levantado is about twenty minutes by boat from the coast. While admittedly just one square kilometer in size, it packs all the advantages of an island paradise into a small area. There are palm-lined bays, white sands, and lush wetland forests. The simple beach restaurants also serve delicious lobster.

Juan Dolio, San Pedro de Macorís (above)

Juan Dolio is a holiday centre on the southern coast of the Dominican Republic. Holidaymakers can saunter along the little promenade in the town centre. Hotels, restaurants, and shops dominate the skyline in the newer part of Juan Dolio. Beautiful Playa Guayacanes is perfectly suited to soaking up the tropical evening atmosphere.

Playa Bacardi, Cayo Levantado (below)

On the heavenly island of Cayo Levantado the natural world seems to take its cue from the script of a rum advert. Palm leaves rock in the wind, casting their fan-like shadows onto the light, powdery sands of Playa Bacardi. This spot was made for sipping rum cocktails and taking in the emerald green ocean.

Playa Juanillo, La Altagracia (above)

Playa Juanillo is just a short ride away by water taxi from it more popular neighbor, Playa de Bavaro. Both are part of the Costa del Coco. At Playa Juanillo, holidaymakers will also find turquoise blue water and a gorgeous sandy beach, as well as a large assortment of restaurants, hotel facilities, and a practically inexhaustible array of leisure and sports activities to suit every taste.

Punta Cana, La Altagracia (lower left)

Punta Cana's success lies in its sugar cane fields, palm groves, fine white sandy beaches, and hotel complexes whose prices often include leisure activities. Given its spacious beaches, visitors can always find a free spot in which to enjoy the sound of the ocean in this tropical paradise on their own.

Isla Saona, La Altagracia (lower right)

A tiny tropical paradise named Isla Saono is sandwiched between turquoise blue water and radiant blue skies. The island lies in the middle of a national park on the southeast coast of the Dominican Republic. One of its main attractions is Piscina Natural, a natural pool where you can stand on a sandy plateau, hip-deep in water, with countless fish swarming all around you.

Bayahibe, La Altagracia *(above)*

Bayahibe Beach in the southeast has a special feature: cool springs spill directly into the sea at this spot, so bathers can splash about in clear fresh water and salty ocean water all at once. Anyone who spent the day in the water can watch red sunsets over the ocean from one of the beach bars in this former fishing village.

Puerto Rico

Escambrón, San Juan *(below)*

San Juan is the capital and tourist centre of the island of Puerto Rico. You can go directly from old town San Juan to the city beach. Escambrón Beach stretches between two rocky capes for 150 m and is protected by an offshore reef. Part of Third Millennium Park, the beach has clear water, and there are lots of bike and walking paths in the park.

The British Virgin Islands

White Bay, Jost van Dyke (above)

Since it lies off the beaten tourist track, White Bay on the island of Jost van Dyke has been able to preserve its charm. There are no big hotels or swanky restaurants. On the other hand, it has beautiful water, a fine sandy beach, and perfect sailing conditions. The island is named after a notorious pirate, and yet the first people to settle here were Quakers.

Cane Garden Bay, Tortola (lower left)

One of the most beautiful anchoring places in the Virgin Islands lies on the main island of Tortola. Gently curving Cane Garden Bay is not only a launching point for sailing trips, but also a favourite place for snorkelling excursions. There are restaurants, bars, sun loungers, and a large selection of shops along the well developed, palm-lined beach.

Lambert Bay, Tortola (lower right)

Until recently, Lambert Bay on the wild, jagged Atlantic Coast was also known as Elizabeth Bay. Green sea turtles lay their eggs here in January and February. Fiery coloured hibiscus bloom here all year long. At the weekend, many locals use the white, palm-fringed beach for long picnics.

Little Dix Bay, Virgin Gorda
(above)

Laurance S. Rockefeller, grandson of the billionaire, discovered Little Dix Bay during a sailing trip and built a posh bungalow hotel on his personal dream bay. Due to its extraordinary beauty, this beach with cliffs and rolling hills has ranked among the world's most perfect travel destinations ever since.

The Baths, Virgin Gorda
(below)

The third largest of the British Virgin Islands is home to the biggest attraction of the archipelago, The Baths. Located at the southern tip of the island, The Baths are a most unusual geological rock formation. Gigantic granite rocks tower near the shore, forming mysterious grottoes that are open to the sea. Together with the sun and blueness of the water, they conjure a breathtaking dose of colour.

The U.S. Virgin Islands

Magen's Bay, St. Thomas
(upper left)

The island of St. Thomas is a frequent destination for cruise ships, and you can circle it in a single day. The Mountain Top near Magen's Bay is the highest vantage point and well worth taking in along the way. From there, visitors get a spectacular panorama of the much-vaunted bay and offshore islands.

Netherlands Antilles

Dawn Beach, Sint Maarten
(upper right)

Sint Maarten belongs to the southern part of the Netherlands Antilles. The hallmarks of this tiny Caribbean island are white palm-lined beaches, turquoise lagoons, and a well developed tourist infrastructure with abundant recreational offerings. Dawn Beach lies on the east coast. Not only is it a nice place for snorkelling, but also an ideal spot for enjoying sunrises and views of St. Barts.

Palm Beach, Aruba
(RH page)

Eagle Beach tends to draw Europeans, whilst adjacent Palm Beach is a favourite holiday spot for Americans. There is an enormous selection of leisure and sports activities on offer. And this wonderfully situated bit of coastline provides visitors with impressive sunsets, as well as several casinos and shopping areas.

Coki Beach, St. Thomas
(below)

Coki Beach in the northeast of St. Thomas offers outstanding snorkelling and diving. The powdery white sand makes it a favourite meeting point for sunworshippers. The main attraction is Coral World, an underwater aquarium that is specially built in the middle of the coral reef. You can look through the peephole at the sea with its abundance of colourful sea creatures.

Guadeloupe
Îlet Pinel, Saint Martin
(above)

Saint Martin, a tiny dream island in the northeastern part of Guadeloupe, has neither electricity nor autos. That's also why it has very clean water, fine sand beaches, and wonderful underwater pathways for snorkelling. Îlet Pinel is a five minute trip by water taxi from the main island of Saint Martin and a must see for day-trippers.

Grand Cul-de-sac, Grand-Terre
(below)

The Grand Cul-de-sac Marine Nature Reserve is located between the main islands of Guadeloupe. This protected area has incredibly white beaches and very impressive fauna and flora. You can silently navigate a pedal boat through the mangrove forests along the coastal areas and take a look at the birds, raccoons, frogs, and beetles that live there.

Petite Terre
(centre/LH page)

Petite Terre's uninhabited islands lie below the eastern tip of Grande-Terre. Scattered about in the sea, you can reach them by motorboat or sailboat. An excursion to the nature reserve and its pristine beaches with ideal snorkelling opportunities comes highly recommended. Furthermore, day-trippers will come upon camera ready wild iguanas.

Sainte Anne, Grand-Terre
(below)

Sainte Anne lies on the east side of Grande-Terre. This is where you'll find the island's loveliest beaches. Once you've left the sugar cane plantations behind, you'll catch sight of a few picture perfect beaches within the flat tropical landscape. The inviting, shimmering turquoise blue water and coral reefs make this a bathing and snorkelling paradise.

Pointe la Feuilliere, Marie Galante *(above)*

Several ferries ply between the main islands and the lush, nearly circular island of Marie Galante. The beach at Pointe la Feuilliere lies in the southeastern part of the island. The crystal clear and coral reef make it an optimal snorkelling spot. Several of the island's rum distilleries and ruins of windmills are also well worth seeing.

Anguilla

Sandy Island *(LH page)*

The Caribbean island of Anguilla is more a spot for serious contemplation than for hustle and bustle. And if you really want to get away from it all, yet still wish to enjoy exuberant Caribbean colours, take a boat trip to Sandy Island. This place has white beaches and pristine snorkelling spots, so plan to enjoy the healing solitude.

Dog Island *(above)*

Dog Island is a tiny coral isle that's easy to get to by motorboat from Anguilla. This dreamy island rises up from the Caribbean waters in every shimmering shade of turquoise. A white strip of sandy beach along the coast and gently breaking waves with green palm trees in the background make Dog Island heaven for Robinsonians.

Shoal Bay *(below)*

The 3 km long beach at Shoal Bay lies in northeastern Anguilla. Its elongated shape led Christopher Columbus to call it Eel Island. Tiny shell particles make the sand radiantly white and shiny, and the sea is wonderfully warm. Lots of Reggae musicians like to play live concerts here. For this reason, Shoal Bay Beach is one of the most popular in the entire Caribbean.

St. Kitts and Nevis

South Friar's Bay, St. Kitts
(above)

No one should leave St. Kitts without having seen South Friar's Bay on the Caribbean side. The most popular beach on the island lies on the leeward side, so it features a calmer ocean that's ideal for swimming and snorkelling. The nearby mangrove forests give shelter to a large number of animals. Monkeys, numerous kinds of birds, and other animals are yours to discover.

Cockleshell Bay, St. Kitts
(upper RH page)

The island's tourist centre, Frigate Bay, lies on a promontory in the southeastern part of St. Kitts. There are intriguing salt lakes and beaches at the southern tip. Cockleshell Bay is a vast beach with golden sand, fantastic bathing, and an impressive view of the spectacular mountainous backdrop of Nevis, the other island in the federation.

Charlestown, Nevis
(lower LH page)

The lush vegetation, quiet beaches, and peaceful atmosphere of Nevis come fairly close to the ideal of a feel-good tropical oasis. Charlestown is the largest city. Marked by clean, tidy streets and eighteenth century colonial buildings, it is one of the oldest, extant cities in the Caribbean.

Pinney's Beach, Nevis
(below)

An extinct volcano dominates the landscape of Nevis. Nevis Peak is usually enveloped in clouds and can be spotted from nearly every location. One of the most beautiful beaches in the region, Pinney's Beach, is known far beyond the borders of this island state. The richly varied landscapes and underwater scenery that surround this heavenly beach probably also contribute to its fame.

Antigua and Barbuda

St. John's, Antigua
(upper left)

The constantly blowing trade winds in the waters around Antigua provide optimal conditions for sailing. Visitors to Antigua and Barbuda can also have fun on holiday by indulging in paragliding, windsurfing, kiteboarding, waterskiing, deep sea fishing, and snorkelling. St. John's is the capital, as well as most happening place on the island.

Dickenson Bay, Antigua
(lower left)

Antigua has 365 beaches from which to choose, one for every day of the year. Dickenson Bay on the northwest coast of Antigua is a veritable tourist's dream. This wonderful seashell beach has fine sand and a well developed infrastructure with bars and water sports on offer. This is the right spot to leave your cares behind whilst gazing at the dramatic skies.

Valley Church Bay, Antigua
(lower RH page)

Valley Church is about twenty minutes away from the capital city, St. John's. It's a picture perfect Caribbean beach with emerald seas, palm trees, and the silhouette of dark green hills. If you can tear yourself away from this heavenly landscape for a moment, you should pay a visit to little Saint John's Cathedral.

Johnson's Point, Antigua
(above)

The beach at Johnson's Point in southeastern Antigua was originally in private hands, but has been a public beach for several years. And a good thing, too! The golden sand is quiet and peaceful, the water laps gently, and the scent of black pineapples wafts on the breeze. A coveted delicacy, this exceptionally sweet sort of pineapple grows only on Antigua.

Dominica

Prince Rupert Bay *(above)*
On the island of Dominica in the Lesser Antilles, nature lovers get their money's worth and then some. High mountain ranges with extinct volcanoes, dense rain forest, hot springs, cascading waterfalls, and steep cliffs are all found within a very small area. The beaches on the northwest coast at Prince Rupert Bay have fine, dark sand and fabulously beautiful coral banks.

Martinique

Anse L'Etang *(lower left)*
Owing to its unusually diverse plant life, countless gardens, plantations, and lush rain forest, Martinique is called the Island of Flowers. Its natural world inspired Paul Gauguin to create impressive paintings. The Caravelle Peninsula is particularly wild and unspoilt, and the beach at Anse L'Etang is a wonderful place to relax in the fine sand.

Les Salines *(lower right)*
Les Salines, one of the loveliest beaches on the isle, lies at Martinique's southern tip. This palm-lined beach is not far from Savane des Petrifications, where you can see the petrified remains of trees. Les Salines offers many opportunities for boat trips. The ocean around the sand banks of Fonds Blancs is breathtakingly beautiful.

St. Lucia

Soufrière *(above)*

The idyllic fishing village of Soufrière is the gateway to St. Lucia's famous landmark, the impressive Pitons. Although the prolific, green tropical vegetation mitigates their steepness, you still cannot climb the 723 and 769 m high peaks via basic hiking trails. They are, therefore, only suitable for experienced rock climbers. But the views are simply breathtaking!

St. Vincent and The Grenadines

Mayreau *(centre)*

Visitors will find a quiet paradise here on the smallest inhabited island in the Grenadines. White sandy beaches, excellent underwater areas, the so-called Mayreau Gardens, and great kitesurfing conditions are its trademarks. Mayreau has a lovely church on a little hill and a small, exclusive hotel.

St. Vincent *(below)*

St. Vincent has been nicknamed the Emerald Isle on account of its lush natural world. Dense rainforest covers the mountainous slopes that go right up to the water. This green island has cascading streams and waterfalls, countless rivers, and even a crater lake. You'll be just as bowled over by brightly coloured underwater world surrounding the island as by the rich tropical flora on land.

Barbados

Paynes Bay *(above)*

Since it's located on the leeward side of this Caribbean island, the waves at Paynes Bay simply ripple on the glassy smooth surface of the water. This beach paradise invites you to swim, sunbathe, or simply dream. Flat beach access and the great variety of water sports on offer make it very popular. Even so, it's not overly crowded.

Crane Bay *(upper RH page)*

If you're looking for a beach that is everything you'd expect of a tropical paradise, then you've found it at Crane Bay on the southern coast of Barbados. This incredibly beautiful bay has lush vegetation, a powdery white beach, and fantastic salt water. It also has impressive waves, plus a heavenly lookout point with views of the sea.

Bathsheba *(below)*

Visitors can give their holiday dreams free reign at this beach. More than 100 km long, it also has a seemingly endless coral reef. Surfers often end up in the fishing village of Bathsheba, which is very popular with their ilk on account of the roaring breakers. This village is a refuge for sophisticated tourists.

Bottom Bay *(below)*

Bottom Bay lies north of Sam Lord's Castle on the southern coast of Barbados. This bay a lesser known paradise of soft sandy beaches, palms, cliffs, and a cave. The beach is surrounded by high cliffs that make it especially picturesque. But the waves can be quite high and unpredictable, so you should exercise caution whilst swimming.

Grenada

Morne Rouge *(above)*

Along with Grand Anse, Morne Rouge is the most important holiday resort on Grenada. Lying in a crescent shaped bay, the beach serves as a drop-in centre for private boats and day-trippers. Heavenly beaches, extinct volcanoes, crater lakes, waterfalls, and nutmeg plantations make Grenada a popular Caribbean tourist destination.

La Sagesse *(lower left)*

The natural surroundings of La Sagesse Bay on the southern coast of Grenada are extraordinarily beautiful. Since the water is calm and shallow, the well-protected, silvery sand beach is an ideal place to swim. The pristine natural setting of lush, exotic flowers, mangrove forests, and aquatic birds along this bit of coastline are an open invitation to hike.

Grand Anse *(lower right)*

At 3 km, Grand Anse Beach is the longest on Grenada. It lies in the middle of the island's main tourist area. The bay is lined with coconut palms. Cruise ship passengers like to come ashore here to enjoy a day at the beach. There are diving schools in Grand Anse Bay, and you can also take boat trips.

Trinidad and Tobago

Maracas Bay, Trinidad *(centre)*

Maracas Bay is Trinidad and Tobago's flagship beach. Its deeply cut bay, surrounded by lush hillsides, looks like a photo mural. Bathers find the golden sand and turquoise water inviting. If you're looking for peace and quiet, then you should come here during the week, because locals really fill it up at the weekend.

Pigeon Point, Tobago *(above)*

Pigeon Point lies in the southwest, which is the most touristically developed area of Tobago. With its blindingly white sand and rows of palms fronds bent low toward the water, Pigeon Point is way up on the list of tropical beaches that have everything. This beach and its beautiful picnic spots are like something out of a picture book. But you must pay a fee to access the private beach.

Parlatuvier Bay, Tobago *(below)*

The little fishing village of Parlatuvier on the Caribbean side of Tobago gets its name from the French expression, *pas le trouver* (EN: can't be found). Far removed from any major resort area, the name still fits this secluded location. A genuine insider's tip: it's wonderfully peaceful and quiet on the fine sand beach, and there's always a chance of spotting nurse or hammer sharks in the clear water.

SOUTH AMERICA

HOT RHYTHMS AND LUST FOR LIFE

Wide plains, impenetrable rain forests, the mighty Amazon river basin, and the magnificent Andes are what make South America a continent of contrasts. This is also true of its coastal areas. And it's not only from the shore that one can experience the unique natural surroundings; the conditions are ideal for divers and water sport enthusiasts, in particular. The Atlantic and Pacific also provide an amazing variety of sea creatures. Penguins, whales, sea lions, elephant seals, and river dolphins all live in South America. Easter Island, a special territory of Chile, is world famous. Scientists have still not solved the riddle of the island's colossal stone figures known as Moai. The isolated Galapagos Islands in the Pacific are another big tourist draw. Penguins and gigantic turtles make their home here. The enchantingly solitary coastlines of the Patagonian wilderness and many faceted dune landscapes of Northern Brazil will captivate you. Beaches to the south, including Rio de Janeiro's Copacabana and the Uruguayan seaside resort of Punta del Este, brim over with activity and lust for life. Collectively, they are living adverts for this richly contrasting continent.

Caribbean Sea

DOMINICA
Guadeloupe

ST. VINCENT AND
THE. GRENADINES
Netherlands Antilles
Martinique
ST. LUCIA
GRENADA
BARBADOS

ATLANTIC

Barranquilla
Maracaibo
Barquisimeto
Caracas
TRINIDAD
AND TOBAGO

PANAMA

VENEZUELA

Medellín

Ciudad
Bolívar

Georgetown

OCEAN

GUYANA

Paramaribo

COLUMBIA

Cali

SURINAME FRENCH
GUIANA

Popayán

Galapagos Islands

ECUADOR

Guayaquil

Iquitos

Santarém

Belém

Fortaleza

Trujillo

Teresina

Natal

Río Branco
Porto Velho

P E R U

B R A Z I L

Callao

BOLIVIA

La Paz
Cochabamba

Rondonópolis

Arequipa

Goiânia

PACIFIC

Iquique

Campo
Grande

Belo Horizonte
Vitória

Antofagasta

Concepción

PARAGUAY

São Paulo

Santos

Paraty

OCEAN

Tucumán

Corrientes

Curitiba

Córdoba

A R G E N T I N A

Rosario

URUGUAY

Pôrto Alegre

Mendoza

Buenos Aires

La Plata

Valparaiso

Santiago

C H I L E

Concepción

Mar del Plata

Valdívia

Bahía Blanca

C. Rivadavia

Falkland Islands

| 0 | 250 | 500 | 750 |
km

Río Gallegos

Punta Arenas

Beaches in South America

1	Johnny Cay, San Andres	12	Jericoacoara, Ceará
2	Viña del Mar	13	Praia do Forte, Bahia
3	Valparaiso	14	Icarai, Niteroi
4	Easter Island	15	Copacabana, Rio de Janeiro
5	Morrocoy National Park	16	Ipanema, Rio de Janeiro
6	Puerto Colombia, Henri Pittier National Park	17	Praia Vermelha, Rio de Janeiro
7	Juan Griego, Isla Margarita	18	Prainha, Rio de Janeiro
8	Playa Pedro Gonzales, Isla Margarita	19	Paraty, Costa Verde
		20	Camburi, São Paulo
9	Playa Medina, Paria	21	Praia Mocambique, Ilha de Santa Catarina
10	Shell Beach, Barima-Waini	22	Punta del Este, Maldonado
11	Îles du Salut		

Columbia

Johnny Cay, San Andres *(above)*

Johnny Cay is an uninhabited island just off Decameron, the main beach in the San Andres Archipelago. Lots of excursion boats head for this idyllic little spot, which is a lovely place for a picnic under the coconut palms. If you're planning to visit this solitary island, you mustn't forget your snorkelling gear, because all manner of rare fish, such as the flying gurnard, live around Johnny Cay.

Chile

Viña del Mar *(below)*

The sophisticated, elegant seaside resort of Viña del Mar lies in the immediate vicinity of Valparaiso. This city of gardens has beautiful parks, immaculate beaches, and dunes. Main attractions of this popular tourist destination include the Flower Clock, Art Deco Casino, and a lookout point from which you can view Valparaiso Bay in its entirety.

Valparaíso *(above)*

The habour city of Valparaíso lies 120 km from the capital, Santiago de Chile. Romantic nooks and crannies, stairways, and lifts are among the reasons that Valparaiso rates among the world's most beautiful cities. The city is located along a perfectly shaped bay with a sandy beach. When they landed in 1536, the Spanish called it "Paradise Valley".

Easter Island *(below)*

A special territory of Chile, Easter Island, lies about 3,500 km off the Chilean coast and remains a mystery to this day. Strewn about the island are gigantic tufa figures that can weigh up to eighty tonnes. As of yet, no one has been able to explain how these ancient statues arrived at their respective locations. The island's only palm-lined beach, Anakena, is a favourite romping spot for windsurfers.

Venezuela

Morrocoy National Park
(upper left)

Situated in northwestern Venezuela, Morro-coy National Park has fine sand islands and a labyrinth of mangrove forests along the coast. A boat trip through the mangroves is a fascinating experience. Visitors should also plan an excursion to Cayo Sombrero, an island with great snorkelling and dazzling coralline beaches.

Puerto Colombia, Henri Pittier National Park *(upper right)*

Playa Grande in Puerto Colombia has pretty much everything that travellers expect of a holiday paradise. Palm trees grow right up to the sparkling, bright green water. If you tire of sun and sand, you can always make a trip to the nearby national park, which is partic-ularly know for its many species of birds.

Juan Griego, Isla Margarita
(below)

The Caribbean island of Margarita lies north-west of the Venezuelan capital, Caracas. Mar-garita is a popular holiday destination that is known for its diverse beaches and perpetual-ly warm water. The holiday resort of Juan Griego lies in the far north. You'll find lots of shops and beach pubs here. When evening comes, the setting sun bathes the entire bay in glowing red light.

Guyana

Playa Pedro Gonzales, Isla Margarita (below)

Playa Pedro Gonzales lies in the northern part of Margarita Island. Framed by hills and cliffs, it's such a pretty spot that you'll want to spend time here. But if you can tear yourself away from the white beach and billowing waves, then we recommend a short excursion to the main town of Porlamar, where holiday guests can shop duty free.

Playa Medina, Paria (above)

The Paria Peninsula has pristine palm-lined beaches, waterfalls, and truly romantic rainforests, all of which make it a really hot tip for travellers. Playa Medina is a magical place in the midst of unadulterated natural surroundings. But if you want to go there, you mustn't expect much in the way of luxury accommodations or recreational options. But the gorgeous beach certainly compensates for lack of same.

Shell Beach, Barima-Waini (upper RH page)

In the language of the indigenous people, Guyana means "land of many waters". And this South American country really does have mighty rivers and waterfalls, as well as wonderful coastal areas. Shell Beach extends along the coast for 140 km. This sandy stretch is known for its wide variety of shells, as well as for sea turtles that perpetually come ashore to lay their eggs between May and July.

French Guiana

Îles du Salut *(below)*

Île Royale is part of a three island archipelago off the coast of French Guiana. This former prisoner's island became world famous on account of the Hollywood film, *Papillon*. The penal colony is long gone. Nowadays, the distinctive characteristics of this island group include countless coconut palms, dense rainforests, and exotic flora and fauna.

Brazil

Jericoacoara, Ceará *(above)*

The long trek to Fortaleza in northern Brazil is well worth the effort. Anyone who comes to Jericoacoara will find himself immersed in a world of lakes, endless sand dunes, and colourful rocks. This enchanting town is called Jeri for short. On account of ideal weather conditions, it is a meeting place for windsurfers and kiteboarders. Beaches in and around Jeri are regularly listed among the world's top ten.

Praia do Forte, Bahia *(centre)*

Praia do Forte lies north of the metropolis of Salvador. To get there, visitors take the Estrada do Coco (EN: Coconut Road). There are beaches lined with coconut palms, lagoons, waterfalls, and a river that has its source in the jungle. The few larger hotels support conservation and protection of the region's sea turtles.

Icarai, Niteroi *(below)*

The little city of Niteroi and Icarai Beach lie in the immediate vicinity of the metropolis at Sugar Loaf. A day trip to the bay is definitely worth your while. If you cross the Rio Niteroi Bridge, you'll escape the flood of tourists. And from Icarai, you'll get a wonderful view of Rio de Janeiro's impressive cityscape and gently rolling hills.

Copacabana, Rio de Janeiro
(above)

Copacabana is renowned for its unique location and sheer vastness. The 4 km long beach lies in the heart of Rio de Janeiro and sits between granite cliffs and the Atlantic Ocean. Many bikini-clad beauties have also added to its celebrity. Brazilians refer to this crescent-shaped beach as the "Little Mermaid".

Ipanema, Rio de Janeiro *(below)*

Ipanema is as much a symbol of Rio as the statue of Christ the Redeemer and neighbouring Copacabana. The rich and famous of Rio de Janeiro meet here in this elegant district and along Ipanema Beach. Up-and-coming footballers and bikini-clad bathing beauties frolic on the beach. And the famous Girls from Ipanema enjoy being seen in the chic bars along the promenade.

Praia Vermelha, Rio de Janeiro
(above)

Praia Vermelha is just the ticket for visitors who wish to escape the chaos of Rio de Janeiro. This small beach between Sugar Loaf and Morro de Leme (EN: Vulture Hill) is relatively unknown to tourists. If you've had enough relaxation, you can always head for the base station behind the beach and take a cable car to Urca Mountain and Sugar Loaf.

Prainha, Rio de Janeiro
(lower left)

Visitors can find peace and quiet outside the big city at Prainha Beach, which is just an hour's drive south of Rio de Janeiro. Lots of surfers come here because of the big waves. The beautiful sandy bay has clean water. There are also shallower stretches of beach, however, that are perfect for bathers. The rainforest begins directly at the back of the bay.

Paraty, Costa Verde
(lower right)

One of Brazil's most beautiful coastlines is found south of Rio. The rainforest reaches all the way to the turquoise blue sea at Costa Verde. A protected historical site, the colonial town of Paraty is among the country's architectural gems. It is surrounded by craggy cliffs, jutting peninsulas, and solitary beaches.

Camburi, São Paulo
(above)

Camburi is a surfing spot in southern Brazil. Bright sands, blue water, and great waves are of special note. Camburi Beach lies amid gently rolling hills and is surrounded by a peninsula. If you'd like to watch the surfers from the beach, you can always stake out a shady spot under one the almond trees.

Praia Mocambique, Ilha de Santa Catarina *(centre)*

Located on Ilha de Santa Catarina in southern Brazil, Florianópolis is a bustling tourist haven. Reasons for its popularity include the elongated bays, fine sandy beaches, and proximity to Uruguay and Argentina. Praia Mocambique is 10 km long and almost undeveloped, so it provides a nice alternative to the busier beaches. Yet it's just stroll away from the action.

Uruguay
Punta del Este, Maldonado
(below)

The location of this exclusive Latin American holiday resort is truly unique: Punta del Este lies on a peninsula of the same name. The peninsula juts out into the Atlantic at the mouth of the Rio de la Plata. And so the western shore faces the river, the eastern one the sea. You'll find bays with calm water, as well as surfing beaches with breakers on the Atlantic side.

AUSTRALIA AND OCEANIA

THE GATES OF PARADISE

Countless islands and islets, including Bora Bora, Tahiti, Rarotonga, Aitutaki, Viti Levu, and Kiribati, are like specks in the endless blue of the Pacific Ocean. Even their names conjure up the Gates of Paradise. As the English poet Rupert Brooke (1887–1915) so aptly put it, "In the South Seas, it seems our Creator has done all in His power to show us what He is capable of". Anyone who sets foot in New Zealand will be gripped by an irrepressible desire to experience the natural world. Snow white peaks, endless beaches, and lush green meadows await winter weary Europeans, who make their escape to the "most beautiful corner of the world". And then there's Australia. The fifth continent offers green rainforests, red deserts, the whitest beaches on Earth, and the legendary Blue Mountains. Anyone travelling Down Under experiences a kaleidoscope of natural wonders. The coastal areas around Sydney, that colourful, bustling metropolis of millions, promise roaring waves, sheer fun and joie de vivre.

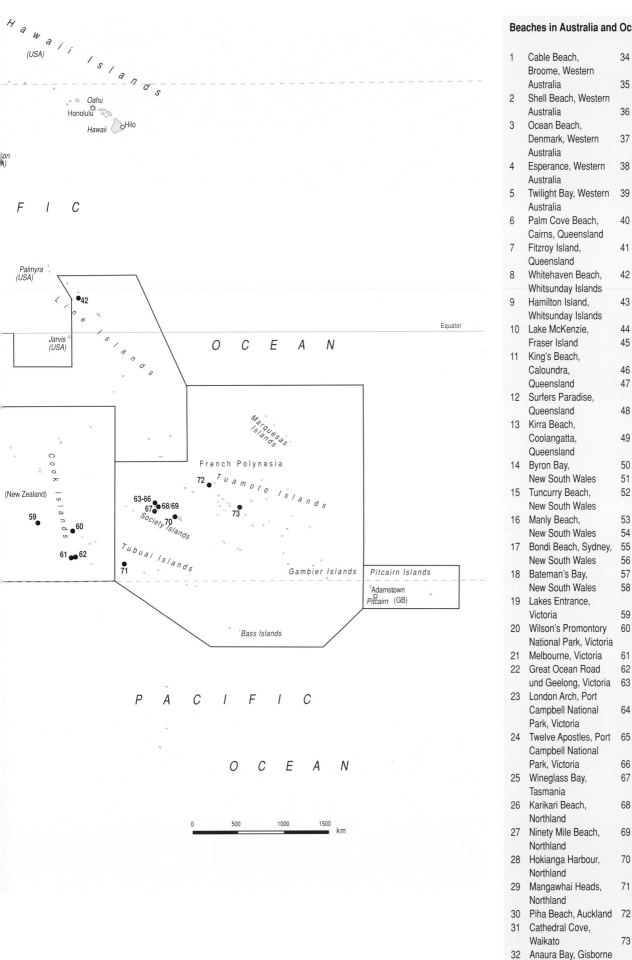

Beaches in Australia and Oceania

1 Cable Beach, Broome, Western Australia
2 Shell Beach, Western Australia
3 Ocean Beach, Denmark, Western Australia
4 Esperance, Western Australia
5 Twilight Bay, Western Australia
6 Palm Cove Beach, Cairns, Queensland
7 Fitzroy Island, Queensland
8 Whitehaven Beach, Whitsunday Islands
9 Hamilton Island, Whitsunday Islands
10 Lake McKenzie, Fraser Island
11 King's Beach, Caloundra, Queensland
12 Surfers Paradise, Queensland
13 Kirra Beach, Coolangatta, Queensland
14 Byron Bay, New South Wales
15 Tuncurry Beach, New South Wales
16 Manly Beach, New South Wales
17 Bondi Beach, Sydney, New South Wales
18 Bateman's Bay, New South Wales
19 Lakes Entrance, Victoria
20 Wilson's Promontory National Park, Victoria
21 Melbourne, Victoria
22 Great Ocean Road und Geelong, Victoria
23 London Arch, Port Campbell National Park, Victoria
24 Twelve Apostles, Port Campbell National Park, Victoria
25 Wineglass Bay, Tasmania
26 Karikari Beach, Northland
27 Ninety Mile Beach, Northland
28 Hokianga Harbour, Northland
29 Mangawhai Heads, Northland
30 Piha Beach, Auckland
31 Cathedral Cove, Waikato
32 Anaura Bay, Gisborne
33 Cape Kidnappers, Hawke's Bay

34 Kahurangi National Park, Tasman
35 Punakaiki, West Coast
36 Three Mile Lagoon, West Coast
37 Haast Beach, West Coast
38 Milford Sound, Southland
39 Moeraki Boulders, Otago
40 Hoopers Inlet, Allan's Beach, Otago
41 Pisamowe Island, Chuuk
42 Fanning Island, Line Islands
43 Kimbe Bay, New Britain
44 Port Vila, Éfaté
45 Île des Pins, Province Sud (South Province)
46 Yasawa Islands
47 Kuata Island, Yasawa Islands
48 Liku Lagoon, Yasawa Islands
49 Malolo Lailai, Mamanuca
50 Tavarua, Mamanuca
51 Viti Levu
52 Homestead Beach, Wakaya
53 Nanuku Levu, Lau
54 Fafa, Tongatapu
55 Port Maurelle, Vava'u
56 Savaii
57 Upolu
58 Two Dollar Beach, Tutuila
59 Palmerston Island
60 One Foot Island, Aitutaki
61 Rarotonga
62 Muri, Rarotonga
63 Motu Tofari, Bora Bora
64 Motu Piti Aau, Bora Bora
65 Motu Tofari, Bora Bora
66 Matira, Bora Bora
67 Tahaa Lagoon, Society Islands
68 Marae Fare Ta, Huahine
69 Pointe Tereva, Huahine
70 Opunohu Bay, Moorea
71 Tubuai, Austral Islands
72 Takapoto, Tuamoto Archipelago
73 Secret Beach, Tuamotu Archipelago

Australia

Ocean Beach, Denmark, Western Australia (upper left)

Denmark lies on the southwest coast of Australia. At present, this former lumberjack town has 2,000 residents. Tropical forests start right at the edge of town. The dune landscapes are fantastic, and the often stormy ocean borders on many heavenly beaches. Beginners learning to surf will find just the right spot at 33 km long Ocean Beach. The waves are long and rolling, the currents ideal.

Shell Beach, Western Australia (upper right)

The blazingly white sands of Shell Beach lie on Australia's west coast. Beginning about 45 km southeast of Denham, this beach at L'Haridon Bight extends along the bay for 110 km. It is one of only two beaches worldwide that consist entirely of shell deposits. The crushed cockle shells form a layer up to 10 m thick.

Cable Beach, Broome, Western Australia (below)

The fascinating little town of Broome in northwestern Australia is an ethnic melting pot of Europeans, Aborigines, indigenous peoples, Japanese, Malaysians, and their respective cultures. And it is at this point that wide, flat Cable Beach stretches for over 20 km along the coast of the crystal clear Indian Ocean – what an impressive bit of fine sand landscape, and not just at sunset!

Esperance, Western Australia
(above)

Esperance is a former gold mining town in southwest Australia. The nearby beaches have snow white sands and turquoise blue water that seem very much like those in the Caribbean. The secluded, fine sand beach in the pristine natural setting of Lucky Bay makes an idyllic spot for a leisurely picnic or swim.

Twilight Bay, Western Australia
(below)

Great Ocean Drive runs westward for 36 km from the little city of Esperance in southwest Australia. Among others, it passes by Twilight Bay Beach, a favorite bathing spot. Visitors will discover a fine sand beach with aquamarine water bordered by smooth granite rocks. The rich array of fish also attracts many anglers.

Palm Cove Beach, Cairns, Queensland *(above)*

Cairns is a regional city in the tropical north. Whilst Cairns makes as an ideal starting point for excursions to the Great Barrier Reef, it also has several beautiful beaches, all of which lie north of the city. One of them, Palm Cove, has snow white sand lined with palm trees. This beach is very much in demand as a honeymoon destination.

Fitzroy Island, Queensland *(below)*

When you head for Fitzroy Island by boat from Cairns, the island looks like a steep hill rising out of the sea. But you can do more than swim and sunbathe on Fitzroy's snow white beaches: the snorkelling in this location by the Great Barrier Reef is also fantastic. And sightings of gorgeous coral and dazzling fish in every imaginable colour are virtually guaranteed.

Whitehaven Beach, Whitsunday Islands *(above)*

Whitehaven Beach is 99.7 % quartz, which makes it the whitest beach on Earth! It lies on uninhabited Whitsunday Island, the largest island in a group of around 90 islands off the east coast of Australia that also go by the same name. Numerous boats make daily excursions to this fascinating, 8 km long beach.

Hamilton Island, Whitsunday Islands *(below)*

Hamilton is the largest inhabited island in the Whitsundays. This 6 km² island has enough room for forested shorelines, sublime hills, and numerous beaches bordering an azure sea. Whilst most of the beaches are quite popular and offer good water sporting opportunities, visitors also come here to hike through the island's unspoilt natural areas.

King's Beach, Caloundra, Queensland (above)

The 60 km long Sunshine Coast begins about an hour's drive north of Brisbane and contains some of Australia's best known beaches. Among them is King's Beach in Caloundra. If you don't feel confident of swimming in the open sea, there is also a separate, salt water pool.

Lake McKenzie, Fraser Island (centre)

Given the white sand and crystal clear, turquoise water, you might feel as if you were in the Caribbean. But McKenzie is a fresh water lake on Fraser Island. The beach is made of pure white silica, which not only looks beautiful, but also acts like a natural scrub and softens your skin.

Byron Bay, New South Wales (below)

The small town of Byron Bay is the most easterly point in Australia. It's equally popular with backpackers and luxury travellers. There are many beaches from which to choose. Main Beach is right in town and ideal for bathing, but surfers prefer Watego's Beach and The Pass. Beaches aside, Byron Bay is famous for its relaxed, alternative lifestyle.

Surfers Paradise, Queensland
(above)

The Gold Coast is a 35 km stretch of coastline on the east coast, and Surfers Paradise is the region's main city. Thanks to the subtropical climate, you can swim and surf here all year long. And Surfers is an adventure-filled town with more than just beaches on offer. It also has numerous hotels, an active nightlife, and amusement parks.

Tuncurry Beach, New South Wales *(below)*

The twin coastal towns of Forster and Tuncurry lie about 220 km north of Sydney on the banks of Wallis Lake. They are especially popular with the locals, who come here to swim, surf, and fish. Many just like to have a weekend away from the chaos of the big city and a bit of fun in the sun. Rockpool is a supervised swimming area at the south end of the beach.

Kirra Beach, Coolangatta, Queensland (above)

One of Australia's most famous surfing beaches, Kirra Beach, is located directly at the border of New South Wales. Lying about 100 km south of Brisbane, its fantastic waves lure countless leisure sports enthusiasts to surf here each year. Point Danger lies on a promontory to the east of the Kirra Beach. From there you'll get a wonderful view of the beach with surfers in action.

Manly Beach, New South Wales (lower left)

Sydney's world famous opera house is located at Circular Key. From here you can also take the half-hour ferry ride to the suburb of Manly. This narrow peninsula on the Pacific has a wonderful beach surrounded by tall Norfolk pines. Manly Scenic Walk heads along the coast for 9 km, offering fantastic panoramas of the beach and ocean.

Bateman's Bay, New South Wales (lower right)

Bateman's Bay lies about 300 km south of Sydney. The little town that was once a fishing harbour is now a favourite day trip destination. Year after year, its snow white silica beaches cast a spell over countless swimmers and surfers. You'll find Murramarang National Park on the nearby coast. And that's where you can get a closer look at Australia's fascinating national animal, the kangaroo.

Bondi Beach, Sydney, New South Wales *(above)*

Bondi Beach, one of the best known and most popular beaches in Australia, is only about fifteen minutes by car from downtown Sydney. Bondi Beach is equally popular among sun worshippers, surfers, and beach volleyball players. In fact, the official 2000 Olympic beach volleyball events took place here. With so many street cafes and restaurants, there's no question that you'll have plenty to do on land, as well as in the water.

Lakes Entrance, Victoria *(below)*

Lakes Entrance is a popular holiday resort and fishing harbour. It gets its name from the canal that links the ocean with the lakes of the Gippsland region. You'll get a fantastic view of the lakes and the mouth of the canal from Jemmy's Point. The golden, gently sloping beach and surrounding dunes at 90 Mile Beach invite you to tarry a bit.

Melbourne, Victoria
(upper left)

Most Australians live no further than one hour from the ocean. The country's second largest city is no exception, and so a whole array of beaches awaits you in Melbourne. The best known of Melbourne's bathing beaches, St. Kilda Beach, is right in town and gets very lively at the weekend. An artist colony has also taken up residence here.

Wilson's Promontory National Park, Victoria *(upper right)*

"Wilson's Prom", as the locals lovingly call this national park, is situated at the southernmost point of the Australian mainland. Nature lovers will find more than 130 km of hiking trails here, plus countless animals, such as koalas, wombats, and even rare Kookaburras. There are also glorious, largely untouched beaches surrounded by lushly forested hills.

Twelve Apostles, Port Campbell National Park, Victoria *(RH page)*

The Twelve Apostles are limestone rocks that tower above the billowing sea for up to 60 m. Despite their name, only eight of them still stand today. These eight are also subject to erosion by wind and rough seas. Twelve Apostles Marine National Park begins here. Its marine world is home to numerous kinds of seahorses, abalone, and sea urchins.

Great Ocean Road and Geelong, Victoria (below)

One of the most impressive coastlines in the world, the Great Ocean Road, runs along the southern coast of Australia. It begins about 70 km west of Melbourne near the city of Geelong and continues westward from there for around 250 km. Wonderful, surfing beaches and dramatic rocky pinnacles along the steep coastline contrast with the green forests of the Otway Ranges.

London Arch, Port Campbell National Park, Victoria (above)

Port Campbell National Park offers incomparable adventures in nature that arguably make it the most frequently photographed section of the Great Ocean Road. There are numerous arches and spectacular rock formations set against breathtaking cliffs. London Arch was originally a natural bridge within Port Campbell National Park. It used to connect a cliff with the mainland, but the arch collapsed in 1990.

Wineglass Bay, Tasmania (below)

The wineglass shaped double bay in Freycinet National Park is located on the east coast of Tasmania. This is where you'll discover white sandy beaches, remote inlets, rocky cliffs, and very well marked hiking trails. Although it takes more than 600 stairs to reach it, Wineglass Bay Lookout will afford you the best view of the white sand bay and crystal clear water.

New Zealand

Ninety Mile Beach, Northland
(upper left)
Ninety Mile Beach at Te Aupouri Peninsula is really a misnomer, because it's actually only 55 miles long. Even so, it is among the country's most important natural wonders. And since it is part of New Zealand's road system, cars are allowed to drive on it. Nevertheless, those seeking relaxation are sure to find enough secluded spots.

Hokianga Harbour, Northland
(upper right)
Hokianga Harbour lies on the northwest coast of the North Island and extends inland from the Tasman Sea for up to 45 km. The coastal region of this natural harbour branches out in all directions. There are mighty sand dunes, white beaches, and dense mangrove forests. The few communities found within its deep inlets are only reachable by boat and are all but cut off from the outside world.

Karikari Beach, Northland
(below)
Doubtless Bay lies in the Northland Region at the tip of the North Island. Captain Cook named it in 1769, reportedly saying that "this is doubtless a bay" (and not an inlet). The Karikari Peninsula extends to the west of the bay. Its dark cliffs and bright sands remains virtually untouched. You can still find plenty of pristine spots amongst its restful dunes.

Mangawhai Heads, Northland
(upper left)

The seaside resort of Mangawhai Heads lies south of the city of Whangarei. The protected bay, an unspoilt sunken estuary in the ocean, is surrounded by an impressive variety of plant life. During the summer months, everything centers around the beach and swimming in the shallow water. With a little luck, bird-watchers will spot *taranui* (Maori for Caspian terns) in the tidelands.

Piha Beach, Auckland
(lower left)

The coastal city of Piha lies 28 km north of Auckland in the Waitakere Ranges. It is a favourite day-trip destination for Auckland residents. Lion Rock divides the beach into northern and southern sections. The rock is 101 m high and looks like a reclining lion. Great swells also make this rugged shoreline a favourite among surfers.

Anaura Bay, Gisborne
(upper RH page)

To reach picturesque Anaura Bay, you take a narrow road off Highway 35. This bay, its golden sands, and big waves enjoy great popularity in the summertime, particularly among surfers. You can also explore the natural surroundings on foot by taking the Anaura Bay Walkway, a pleasant 3.5 km long hiking trail through the green hills.

Cathedral Cove, Waikato
(below)

Cathedral Cove is a bay on the Coromandel Peninsula of New Zealand's North Island. It is surrounded by bright limestone rocks that rise out of the sea for up to 40 m. The bay got its name from a cave whose vaulted ceiling is reminiscent of a cathedral. The marine reserve of the same name is home to a variety of perch, as well as crabs and sea anemones.

Cape Kidnappers, Hawke's Bay
(above)

The coastal cliffs of Cape Kidnappers tower loftily out of the sea. The beaches here are made of the most finely textured gravel, and parts of them can only be traversed at low tide. The name of the promontory derives from an event that took place in 1769: Maoris apparently tried and failed to abduct the servant of a crew member from Captain Cooks' vessel, HMS Endeavour. Today the cape is mainly known for its large colony of gannets.

Punakaiki, West Coast
(below)

The beach in the small town of Punakaiki lies at the edge of Paparoa National Park. The views from here are impressive, especially at sunset. It has a forested coastline and a rock towering up from the ocean that you can walk on at low tide. Thousands of seabirds nest in the area each year. A large colony of black Westland petrels makes its home south of the Punakaiki River.

Kahurangi National Park, Tasman (above)

Kahurangi National Park lies in the northwestern part of the South Island. The sheer diversity of the natural environment will astound you. There are forested plateaus in the uplands and highlands, and mighty mountain ranges like the Mount Arthur Range. You'll find peaceful valleys like the Karamea River Valley, as well as Scotts Beach and others like it, framed by green hills and unspoilt rocky coastlines. This is the starting point of the 82 km long Heaphy Track, one of the most popular hiking trails in New Zealand.

Haast Beach, West Coast (below)

The little town of Haast lies near the spot where the Haast River flows into the Tasman Sea. The area is home to a great many seals, as well as one of the largest colonies of thick-billed penguins in the world. The beach itself will captivate you with its primeval natural surroundings, puffy sand dunes, and inland lagoons. Although the species is endangered, there are still a few North Island Brown Kiwis here.

Milford Sound, Southland
(above)

Milford Sound lies on New Zealand's South Island. The English writer Rudyard Kipling described it as the "eighth wonder of the world". And once you've seen this fjord, you will surely remember it all your life. Reaching inland from the Tasman Sea, the rocky walls on the banks of this 15 km wide sound rise to heights of more than 1,200 m.

Three Mile Lagoon, West Coast
(below)

Stretching from New Zealand's Southern Alps to the wild sea coast, Westland Tai Poutini National Park spans an area of 1,175 km². In a relatively narrow area, you'll find mighty glaciers, atmospheric lakes, temperate rain-forests, the remains of gold rush towns, and beach after wonderful, deserted beach like the one at Three Mile Lagoon.

Hoopers Inlet, Allan's Beach, Otago *(above)*

The Otago Peninsula extends to the northeast of Dunedin for 35 km. Hoopers Inlet is about half way between Dunedin and the tip of the peninsula. The golden sands of Allan's Beach can only be reached on foot. Penguins nest in the impressive dunes, and the sunsets are magnificent. With a bit of luck, you may even catch sight of a sea lion.

Moeraki Boulders, Otago *(below)*

The Moeraki Boulders rest like marbles on Koekohe Beach about 40 km south of Oamaru. These spherical blocks of stone can be up to 2.20 m in diameter. According to Maori legend, they are bottle gourds that fell from the mythical canoe Areiteuru when it ran aground here. Since then, these stones have lent a magical, fairytale-like character to these lonesome shores.

Papua New Guinea

Kimbe Bay, New Britain *(above)*

Vast Kimbe Bay is distinguished by immense biodiversity within a relatively small area. About sixty percent of all Indo-Pacific coral species are found here. In addition, there are more than 860 species of tropical reef fish. The overwhelming sunsets and secluded beaches are also quite an experience.

Micronesia

Pisamowe Island, Chuuk *(lower left)*

Chuuk is an atoll in the Caroline Islands, an archipelago in Oceania. Along with another 2,000-plus islands and atolls, it is part of Micronesia. In total, Chuuk consists of eleven mountainous islands surrounded by a few small isles, a barrier reef, and flowing, crystal clear water. During the course of its checkered history, this group of islands has been under Spanish, German, and Japanese rule.

New Caledonia

Île des Pins, South Province *(lower right)*

Île des Pins (EN: Isle of Pines) calls itself "the nearest isle to Paradise". This 15 km long, 13 km wide island lies southwest of Grande Terre, the main island of New Caledonia. A former French penal colony, the island's thickly forested hills and snow white sandy beaches make it a present day paradise for snorkellers, who can explore tropical fish and colourful coral in its crystal clear lagoons.

Vanuatu

Port Vila, Éfaté *(above)*

Vanuatu is an island nation consisting of eighty-three mountainous volcanic islands. Port Vila, the capital of Vanuatu, lies on the southern coast of the island of Éfaté. About 40,000 people currently live in this seaport. Numerous cruise ships and mercantile vessels dock here each day, most of them from New Zealand and Australia. But you can also watch the sunsets from the harbour on a sailboat or small excursion boat.

Kiribati

Fanning Island, Line Islands *(below)*

Fanning Island is a dreamy South Sea atoll with an oval lagoon. It is named after the American explorer Edmund Fanning. But the locals call it Tabuaeran. There are a great many coconut palms growing on the island. So it is that the 2,500 residents of the island live mostly from the production of copra, the dried meat of the coconut that is used in the production of coconut oil.

Fiji

Yasawa Islands
(upper left)

The Yasawa Group, an archipelago in the Western Division of Fiji, consists of twenty volcanic islands in all. They have only been open to the public since 1978, and you still need permission to visit them nowadays. Peaceful bays, emerald green seas, and breathtaking reefs add to the charm of this Pacific paradise. These islands and their enchanting lagoons became famous as the setting for the Hollywood film, *The Blue Lagoon*.

Kuata Island, Yasawa Islands
(below)

Kuata belongs to the Yasawa Group, and it's an island paradise if there ever was one. Climbing the rocky hills at the centre of this little island is well worth the effort. From there you'll get a fantastic view of Waya Island to the north. You can cool off in the lagoon afterwards or enjoy the breathtaking sunsets whilst sitting on the beach in the evening.

Liku Lagoon, Yasawa Islands
(upper RT/LH page)

Like pearls on a string, the Yasawa Islands stretch for 180 km across the wide expanse of the South Sea. Liku Lagoon is also located here, and you may well discover jacks, butterfly fish, and garfish in its coral reefs. The solitary, white beaches are purely for relaxation.

Malolo Lailai, Mamanuca
(above)

Fiji is an island nation in the South Pacific. The archipelago consists of around 322 islands and 522 islets. One of the islands, Malolo Lailai, has - would you believe it? - twelve glorious beaches on offer. Anyone who can't decide on a beach can still enjoy the finer things in life by strolling through the island's lush gardens and coconut plantations.

Tavarua, Mamanuca
(below)

The South Sea paradise of Tavarua lies at the southwestern edge of Fiji's barrier reef. Surrounded by a coral reef, this densely forested island is lined with fine sandy beaches. Anglers and divers will find tuna and mahi mahi in the abundant fishing grounds. This heart shaped island also has fantastic, deep blue waves and a large, enthusiastic following among surfers.

Viti Levu
(upper left)

You'll find a few of the South Pacific's most spectacular beaches on Viti Levu, including Natadolo Beach, Korotongo Beach, and Pacific Harbor. At 10,390 km², Viti Levu is Fiji's largest island. The nation's capital, Suva, is also located here. This island offers plenty of opportunity to sit beneath a palm and experience fascinating sunsets over the volcanic islands.

Homestead Beach, Wakaya
(upper right)

There are over thirty pristine beaches on the private island of Wakaya, and Homestead Beach is among them. This white sandy beach is the longest on the island. Its crystal clear waters are home to yellow puffer fish. You can take extensive hikes through the rainforest and visit archeological sites that date back to 700 BCE.

Nanuku Levu, Lau
(below)

Nanuku Levu is located in the Northern Lau group. In 2002, three New Zealanders leased the island for a period of 99 years. With snow white sands, coconut palms, and a coral reef where sea turtles cavort, this island has every chance of becoming a true island paradise.

Tonga

Port Maurelle, Vava'u *(above)*

The first European to set foot on the Vava'u Archipelago was the Spanish explorer Don Francisco Antonio Maurelle. He dropped anchor here in 1781 and gave his name to Port Maurelle. This archipelago has peaceful, coral sand beaches. You'll be captivated by the forested hills and impressive reefs with magnificent starfish and Pacific mussels.

Fafa, Tongatapu *(below)*

Fafa lies offshore from Tonga's main island of Tongatapu. Sandy beaches line this coral island, which is covered in palm trees. The island's natural beauty remains largely untouched, such that you can find numerous secluded beaches. The surrounding coral reef makes the crystal clear waters of the lagoon safe for swimming and snorkelling.

American Samoa

Two Dollar Beach, Tutuila *(above)*

Tutuila, the largest island in the unincorporated territory of American Somoa, has a large natural harbour. And that is where the capital, Pago Pago, is located. Two Dollar Beach lies in the western part of the city. Since this is a private beach, visitors must pay an entrance fee of two dollars. But the price is well worth it, because you can enjoy a pleasant swim in the calm water, snorkel near shore, or just lie in the sun and take it easy.

Samoa

Upolu *(lower LH page)*

Upolu is the main island in the State of Samoa. This former volcano boasts lush tropical vegetation, as well as a large number of rivers, streams, and waterfalls. The beaches are picture perfect, and Return to Paradise Beach is no exception. Located on the western side of the island, it got its name from the Gary Cooper film of the same name.

Savaii *(below)*

"The soul of Samoa" is what they call the larger of the two main islands in the Independent State of Samoa. Savaii was formed by an active volcano that rose out of the western Pacific. The last time it erupted was in 1911. Unlike the neighbouring island of Upolu, Savaii is relatively quiet and secluded. But you will still find fabulous beaches, as well as trumpet fish and a colourful marine world.

The Cook Islands

One Foot Island, Aitutaki *(above)*

Aitutaki is one of the Cook Islands. Above all, the island is famous for its turquoise lagoon, palm-lined beaches, and the many little uninhabited islands in the immediate vicinity. One of them, One Foot Island, lies in the southeastern part of the lagoon. Not only will you find one of the loveliest beaches in the world on this footprint shaped island; you'll also get a fantastic view of the entire lagoon from there.

Palmerston Island *(below)*

This coral atoll is located about 500 km northwest of Rarotonga. James Cook discovered it in 1774. Palmerston Atoll encompasses a group of sand islands that skirt around coral reef, and the reef in turn encircles a lagoon. The bathing beaches on these islands have powdery white sands. Coconut palms thrive here. But it's only possible to access the islands at a few points where small boats can navigate the reefs.

Rarotonga *(upper RH page)*

Rarotonga is the most populous of the Cook Islands. The island's population stands at 9,500, and the national capital, Avarua, is also located here. This island's endless beaches and superb water sport opportunities make it a favourite holiday destination. Yet despite its popularity, it has remained pristine. Dense rainforests and volcanic peaks dominate the interior. One of the peaks, Te Rua Manga, stands at 658 m.

Muri, Rarotonga *(below)*

The lagoon on the island of Rarotonga extends for several hundred metres and goes all the way out to the coral reef in some places. The reef surrounds nearly the entire island and drops off precipitously into deep water. The widest and deepest lagoon is located in the southeastern part of the island around wide, sandy Muri Beach. The shimmering turquoise waters of the lagoon are especially lovely for swimming, snorkelling, and canoeing.

French Polynesia

Motu Tofari, Bora Bora *(above)*

The natural surroundings on the volcanic island of Bora Bora are famous for their evocative island ambience. Picnics are a favourite on the motus, which are palm-lined coral islets strewn about in the turquoise blue waters off Bora Bora. Motu Tofari is one of them: the wonderful beaches and crystal clear, shallow waters of this romantic islet are most alluring.

Motu Tapu, Bora Bora
(upper RH page)

The tiny island of Motu Tapu lies a few hundred metres west of Bora Bora and is one of the most photographed islands in the South Seas. Its snow white beach, picturesque coconut palms, and crystal clear turquoise blue water make Motu Tapu the epitome of a tropical paradise. But not everyone has access to this particular Eden: only guests from a few select hotels may visit Motu Tapu.

Matira, Bora Bora *(below)*

The loveliest beaches in the South Seas are located at the southern tip of Bora Bora. Matira is a little bit of heaven, radiating natural perfection and cheerful serenity. The sky-blue waters and fine sandy beach make the bay a popular choice as a honeymoon destination for newlyweds. But it's perfect for anyone who wants to enjoy a bit of romance in the South Seas.

Motu Piti Aau, Bora Bora *(below)*

The name Motu Piti Aau means "two hearts", and the sight of this island really will make your heart beat faster. This coral island east of Bora Bora will entice you with its turquoise blue lagoon, white sands, lush tropical vegetation, and wonderful view of Mount Otemanu on the main island. Lots of sea turtles splash about in the waters around the island.

Pointe Tereva, Huahine *(centre/LH page)*

The best way to see the volcanic island of Hauhine is from the water on an excursion boat. The jagged inlets and snow white beaches, among them Pointe Tereva, will simply take your breath away. The interior of the island and the well-preserved archaeological ritual sites at the village of Maeva, in particular, are well worth visiting.

Marae Fare Ta, Huahine *(above)*

Although a sandbar connects them at low tide, Hauhine actually consists of two separate islands. They are surrounded by heavenly white beaches and a blue lagoon. Along with lots of other islets, Huahine lies within a coral reef. A river flows through the island, and eels up to 1.80 m long live in its waters. These creatures are sacred to Polynesians. You can watch them from a nearby bridge.

Tahaa Lagoon, Society Islands *(lower left)*

The island of Tahaa and its lagoon look almost unreal from the air. The lagoon shimmers in countless shades of blue that run the gamut from turquoise to sapphire. Numerous orchid plantations exude a constant scent of vanilla, which is why they also call it "Vanilla Island". You'll get a glorious view of Bora Bora from the white beach, which is framed coconut palms, hibiscus, and flowering grasses.

Opunohu Bay, Moorea *(lower right)*

The towering mountains on the island of Moorea are reflected in the dark waters of Opunohu Bay. The bay lies on the northwest coast of the island. Its fine sand beach and quiet lagoon provide a delightful contrast to the wild, green mountain ranges. The lush vegetation has made this Island of Flowers a preferred setting for lots of South Seas films.

Takapoto
(above)

Takapoto Atoll, its mighty coconut palms, sandy beaches and crystal clear, turquoise lagoon make many a South Seas dream come true. The rare, black pearl, known as the jewel of the South Seas, was first cultured on this island. And you can still visit numerous pearl farms on Takapoto today.

Secret Beach, Tuamotu Archipelago *(lower left)*

Anyone arriving at Secret Beach may well think he's stepped into an idyllic painting. Secret Beach lies east of the Society Islands in the Tuamotu Archipelago. This archipelago in the South Pacific is the largest group of coral atolls in the world. It consists of seventy-eight picturesque atolls and countless individual islands, making it the ideal spot for modern day Robinson Crusoes to find their very own island.

Tubuai, Austral Islands
(lower right)

The palm-lined beaches and luminous, silvery South Sea waves of Tubuai provided the setting for Mutiny on the Bounty. The mutineers, led by Fletcher Christian, actually did try to settle on the island in 1789. They founded Fort George on the north coast. But their efforts failed, due to clashes with the natives.

Index

Photo credits

a. = above
b. = below
l. = left
r. = right

dpa Picture-Alliance GmbH:

P. 5; 6 l., r.; 7 a.l., a.r., b.l.; 8/9; 12 a.; 13 b.; 14 M., b.; 15 (2); 16 a.l.; 17 b.; 18/19 (4); 20/21 (5); 22 b.; 23 (2); 24 (2); 25 b.; 26 b.; 28 a., M.; 29; 30 a.l., b.; 31 b.; 32 b.; 33 (2); 34 (2); 35 b.; 36 (2); 37 b.; 38 a., b.; 39 (2); 40/41 (5); 42 (2); 43 a.; 44/45 (5); 46 b.; 47 (3); 48 M., b.; 49 (2); 50 a., M.; 51 (2); 52 (2); 53 a.; 54/55 (5); 56 a.; 57 b.; 58/59 (3); 60 b.r.; 61 a.; 62 (2); 63 a.; 64/65 (5); 66/67 (5); 68/69 (4); 70 (3); 71 b.l., b.r.; 72 a.r., b.; 73 (2); 74 (3); 76/77 (5); 78 a., M.; 79 (2); 80/81 (5); 82 (2); 83 a.r., b.; 84/85 (5); 86/87; 90/91 (4); 92 b.; 93 b.; 94 b.l., b.r.; 95 a., b.l.; 97 (2); 98 a.; 99 (2); 100 a.l.; 101 b.; 102 b.; 104 a.; 105 (3); 106 a.; 107 a.; 109 b.; 110 (3); 111 b.; 112/113; 115 a., b.l., b.r.; 116/117 (5); 118 (3); 119 a.; 122 a.; 123 (3); 124 a.; 125 (3); 127 (3); 128 b.; 129 (2); 130 (2); 131 b.; 132/133 (5); 137 (2); 138 (2); 140 a., b.l.; 141 a.; 142 a.; 143 b.; 144 a., b.r.; 145 a.; 146/147 (5); 148 a., b.r.; 149 b.; 150 (3); 151 a.; 153 a.l., b.; 154/155 (5); 156 a.; 157 (2); 158/159 (4); 160 (2); 161 b.; 162 (2); 163 a.; 165 (3); 166/167 (5); 168/169; 172/173 (4); 174/175 (5); 176 b.; 177 a.l., a.r.; 178 a.; 179 a., M.; 180/181 (4); 182/183 (4); 184/185 (5); 186/187 (5); 188/189 (4); 190/191 (5); 192/193 (3); 194/195 (4); 196/197 (4); 198/199 (6); 200 (2); 201 a.; 202 (3); 203 b.; 207 (2); 208 a.; 209 (3); 210/211 (4); 212 (3); 213 b.; 214 b.l., b.r.; 215 (3); 216/217; 220/221 (5); 222/223 (4); 224 a., b.; 225 (2); 226/227 (5); 228/229 (4); 230/231 (5); 232/233 (4); 234/235 (4); 236 (2); 237 a.; 238/239 (5); 240 (3); 241 b.; 244 a.; 245; 246/247 (4); 248/249 (5); 250 b.l., b.r.; 251 a., b.r.

Interfoto:

P. 7 b.r.; 12 b.; 13 a., M.; 14 a.; 16 a.r., b.; 17 a.; 25 a.; 26 a., M.; 27 b.; 28 b.; 30 a.r.; 31 a.; 32 a.; 35 a.; 37 a.; 38 M.; 43 b.; 46 a.; 48 a.; 56 b.; 60 a., b.l.; 61 b.; 63 b.; 71 a.; 72 a.l.; 75; 92 a.l., a.r.; 93 a.; 94 a.; 95 b.r.; 96 (2); 98 b.; 100 a.r., b.; 101 a.; 102 a.; 103 (2); 104 b.; 106 b.; 107 b.; 108; 109 a.; 115 M.; 119 b.; 120/121 (5); 122 b.; 124 b.; 128 a.; 131 a.; 141 b.; 142 M.; 143 a.; 144 b.l.; 145 b.; 149 a.; 152; 153 a.r.; 156 b.; 161 a.; 163 b.; 164; 176 a.; 177 b.; 178 b.; 179 b.; 201 b.; 203 a.; 204/205; 213 a.; 214 a.; 237 b.; 241 a.; 242/243 (5); 244 b.; 250 a.; 251 b.l.

mauritius images GmbH:

P. 6 M.; 22 a.; 27 a.; 50 b.; 53 b.; 57 a.; 78 b.; 83 a.l.; 106 M.; 111 a.; 126; 134/135; 139 (2); 140 b.r.; 142 b.; 148 b.l.; 151 b.; 203 M.; 208 b.; 224 M.